A gift from:
Friends of the
Pinole Library

EXPLORERS
AND
EXPLORATION

LEIF ERIKSSON – NATURAL RESOURCES

Marshall Cavendish
New York • London • Singapore

Marshall Cavendish
99 White Plains Road
Tarrytown, New York 10591-9001

www.marshallcavendish.com

Consultants: Ralph Ehrenberg, former chief, Geography
and Map Division, Library of Congress, Washington, DC;
Conrad Heidenreich, former historical geography
professor, York University, Toronto; Shane Winser,
information officer, Royal Geographical Society, London

Contributing authors: Dale Anderson, Kay Barnham,
Peter Chrisp, Richard Dargie, Paul Dowswell, Elizabeth
Gogerly, Steven Maddocks, John Malam, Stewart Ross,
Shane Winser

MARSHALL CAVENDISH
Editor: Thomas McCarthy
Editorial Director: Paul Bernabeo
Production Manager: Michael Esposito

WHITE-THOMSON PUBLISHING
Editors: Alex Woolf and Steven Maddocks
Design: Ross George and Derek Lee
Cartographer: Peter Bull Design
Picture Research: Glass Onion Pictures
Indexer: Fiona Barr

ISBN 0-7614-7535-4 (set)
ISBN 0-7614-7541-9 (vol. 6)

Printed in China

08 07 06 05 04 5 4 3 2 1

color key	time period
▬▬▬▬	to 500
▬▬▬▬	500–1400
▬▬▬▬	1400–1850
▬▬▬▬	1850–1945
▬▬▬▬	1945–2000
▬▬▬▬	general articles

Library of Congress Cataloging-in-Publication Data
Explorers and exploration.
    p. cm.
  Includes bibliographical references (p.) and index.
  ISBN 0-7614-7535-4 (set : alk. paper) -- ISBN 0-7614-
7536-2 (v. 1) -- ISBN 0-7614-7537-0 (v. 2) -- ISBN 0-7614-
7538-9 (v. 3) -- ISBN 0-7614-7539-7 (v. 4) -- ISBN 0-7614-
7540-0 (v. 5) -- ISBN 0-7614-7541-9 (v. 6) -- ISBN 0-7614-
7542-7 (v. 7) -- ISBN 0-7614-7543-5 (v. 8) -- ISBN 0-7614-
7544-3 (v. 9) -- ISBN 0-7614-7545-1 (v. 10) -- ISBN 0-
7614-7546-X (v. 11)
  1. Explorers--Encyclopedias. 2. Discoveries in
geography--Encyclopedias. I. Marshall Cavendish
Corporation. II. Title.
  G80.E95 2005
  910'.92'2--dc22

                        2004048292

CONTENTS

LEIF ERIKSSON

THE NORSE NAVIGATOR AND CHRISTIAN MISSIONARY Leif Eriksson lived at the start of the second millennium CE and is thought by many historians to have been the first modern European to set foot on the continent of North America.

Right **This modern statue of Leif Eriksson, which accords with the description in the sagas of a man "big and strong, of striking appearance," stands in Reykjavik, Iceland.**

THE WRITTEN EVIDENCE

The exploits of Leif Eriksson are recorded in two sagas (heroic family histories unique to Norse literature) written in Iceland in the thirteenth century. As the *Saga of Erik the Red* and the *Saga of the Greenlanders* were written some two hundred years after the events they describe and in some parts contradict each other, it is not easy to piece together an accurate picture of Eriksson's life and deeds.

EARLY LIFE

Born around 970 in Iceland, Eriksson was the son of the Norse explorer Erik the Red. When he was eight, he went to live with Tyrkir, a German who lived in Iceland. Tyrkir taught Eriksson to read and write and to use weapons. Around 982 Eriksson's father committed a murder and was banished from Iceland. The family sailed west to Greenland, where, sometime during the 980s, Erik the Red established colonies for Norse settlers.

According to the *Saga of Erik the Red*, in about 999 Eriksson left Greenland on a voyage bound for Norway. However, a storm blew his ship off course to the Hebrides, a group of islands that lie to the west of Scotland, where Eriksson spent the summer. By the end of the year, Eriksson was in Norway, where he met King Olaf Tryggvason (reigned 995–1000), Norway's first Christian monarch.

King Olaf converted Eriksson to Christianity, and in the following year, 1000, Eriksson prepared his ship for the return journey to Greenland, with instructions from the king to

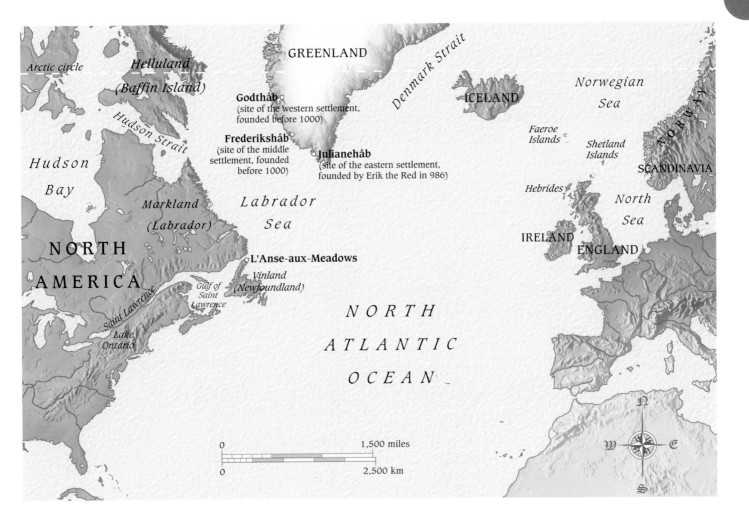

Arctic circle
Helluland
(Baffin Island)
GREENLAND
Denmark Strait
ICELAND
Norwegian Sea
NORWAY

Hudson Strait
Godthåb
(site of the western settlement, founded before 1000)
Faeroe Islands
Shetland Islands
SCANDINAVIA

Hudson Bay
Frederikshåb
(site of the middle settlement, founded before 1000)
Julianehåb
(site of the eastern settlement, founded by Erik the Red in 986)

Markland
(Labrador)
Labrador Sea
Hebrides
North Sea

NORTH AMERICA
IRELAND
ENGLAND

L'Anse-aux-Meadows
Vinland (Newfoundland)

Gulf of Saint Lawrence
Saint Lawrence
Lake Ontario

NORTH ATLANTIC OCEAN

0 ———— 1,500 miles
0 ———— 2,500 km

convert the Greenlanders to Christianity. For Olaf, spreading the Christian faith was a means of strengthening his hold over his people and vast territories. By agreeing to take the Christian message to Greenland, Eriksson acted as Olaf's missionary.

JOURNEY TO A NEW WORLD

Eriksson never reached Greenland. The *Saga of Erik the Red* tells how his ship was blown off course and taken past Greenland to an unknown land far to the west—which has been identified by many historians as North America. After spending the winter there, Eriksson returned to Greenland, taking with him the wild wheat and grapes that he had discovered. According to the *Saga of Erik the Red*, Eriksson rescued a group of fellow Norse sailors shipwrecked on the North American coast—an act that earned him the nickname Leif the Lucky. Yet this saga is generally considered to be a work of fiction, designed to place more emphasis on the role of a later Norse explorer, Thorfinn Karlsefni.

Above **Leif Eriksson reached North America around 1000, after being blown off course when he was sailing from Norway to Greenland.**

c. 970
Leif Eriksson is born in Iceland.

c. 982
Is taken to Greenland by his father, Erik the Red.

c. 999
Sails from Greenland to Norway.

c. 1000
Sets out for Greenland on a mission to convert the Greenlanders to Christianity; is blown off course and lands in North America.

c. 1002
Returns to Greenland.

c. 1020
Dies in Greenland.

Latitude Sailing

During their crossings of the Atlantic, Norse seafarers were out of sight of land for several days at a time. Norse navigators may have used a method known as latitude sailing. Having noted the angle of the North Star above the horizon at their home port, the navigator plotted a course to the west that kept this angle constant until landfall was reached. The ship would then hug the coast as it sailed north or south. For the journey home, a navigator would simply return to the point on the foreign shore where the angle of the North Star matched that at the home port before sailing east—once again, on a course that kept this angle constant. Transatlantic explorers of the fifteenth and early sixteenth centuries, such as John Cabot and his son Sebastian, also plotted their courses by latitude sailing.

NAMING THE NEW WORLD

The *Saga of the Greenlanders* gives a different version of events. According to that saga, around the year 1000 Eriksson sailed west from Greenland with thirty-five men. His goal was to search for the land sighted some fourteen years previously by Bjarni Herjolfsson, an Icelandic merchant and navigator. Herjolfsson had reported the existence of large woodlands, and Eriksson aimed to return with a cargo of timber—a scarce resource on Greenland.

Eriksson's first landfall was at a place of bare rock and glaciers, which has been identified as present-day Baffin Island. He named it

Helluland, meaning "flatstone land." From there he sailed south to a low-lying land covered in forests, which he named Markland ("wood land," present-day Labrador). Farther south he came to a land with a mild climate, rivers stocked with salmon, and an abundance of wild grapes—for which he gave it the name Vinland ("wine land"). Vinland is probably present-day Newfoundland.

According to the *Saga of the Greenlanders*, Eriksson and his fellow travelers wintered in Vinland, where they constructed shelters and explored areas away from the coast. In 1002 they returned to Greenland with timber for the island's colonists.

The following excerpt describes Leif Eriksson's arrival in North America:

. . . They sailed up to the land, cast anchor, and launching a boat, went ashore. They saw no grass; the interior was all great glaciers, and from these to the shore the land looked like one flat rock . . . Leif said: ". . . I will call this land Helluland." They returned to the ship, put out to sea, and found a second land. They sailed to the land, anchored, launched a boat, and went ashore. This was a level wooded land with broad stretches of white sand sloping down to the sea. Leif said: "This land shall have a name after its nature; we will call it Markland." . . . and when the spring came they made their ship ready and sailed away; and from the products [of the third land they visited] Leif gave it a name and called it Vinland.

Saga of the Greenlanders

ERIKSSON'S LEGACY

Leif Eriksson never returned to North America, but his pioneering voyage offered conclusive proof of the existence of land west of Greenland. His voyages inspired other Norse explorers to visit the continent, including Leif's brother Thorvald, his sister Freydis, and Thorfinn Karlsefni, whose colonizing expedition in about 1009 may have resulted in the Norse settlement at L'Anse aux Meadows (excavated by archaeologists in the 1960s). Confusingly, the *Saga of Erik the Red* claims that it was Karlsefni who gave the names Helluland, Markland, and Vinland to areas of North America—that is, the very names apparently chosen by Eriksson a few years earlier.

Eriksson spent the rest of his life on Greenland, where he inherited his father's land and became the leader of the island's community of Norse settlers. He died there around 1020.

Left **This nineteenth-century American painting offers a rather fanciful impression of Leif Eriksson's arrival in America. It depicts Viking soldiers disembarking from a long ship (a war vessel), whereas Eriksson's expedition of merchants probably traveled on a type of cargo ship known as a** *knarr.*

SEE ALSO
• Erik the Red • Gudrid • Vikings

Lewis and Clark Expedition

AS YOUNG OFFICERS IN THE U.S. ARMY, Captain Meriwether Lewis (1774–1809) and Lieutenant William Clark (1770–1838) were given command of the Corps of Discovery, which was set up by President Thomas Jefferson in 1803. On an expedition that lasted two years and four months, they covered almost eight thousand miles of the territory that lay to the west of the land then held by the United States. Their maps of the Missouri and Columbia river systems helped to open up the western frontier, and the record of their journey remains one of the most informative and lively accounts of the American West as it was before it was settled by people of European descent.

Right **When Thomas Jefferson took office in 1801, most U.S. citizens lived within fifty miles (80 km) of the Atlantic Ocean. The rapid westward spread of American influence was sparked by Jefferson's vision of a territory that stretched to the Pacific Ocean.**

By the beginning of the nineteenth century, the settlements originally established by European colonists in the sixteenth and seventeenth centuries had grown considerably. Nevertheless, the people of the United States of America, which had won independence in 1776, knew little of the land that lay more than a few hundred miles from the eastern coast and little of the people who lived there.

In 1801 President Thomas Jefferson was inspired by accounts of the successful expeditions of Alexander Mackenzie in western Canada. Fearing that the British might seek to gain control of the lands that lay west of the Mississippi River, Jefferson asked his secretary, Meriwether Lewis, to lead an expedition to explore the vast territory that separated the United States from the Pacific Ocean.

1770
William Clark is born.

1774
Meriwether Lewis is born.

FEBRUARY 28, 1803
Lewis is given command of an expedition to explore the West.

APRIL 30, 1803
Under the terms of the Louisiana Purchase, President Jefferson buys a huge swath of North America from Emperor Napoleon.

MAY 14, 1804
Lewis and Clark expedition sets out from Saint Louis, Missouri.

OCTOBER 24, 1804
Lewis and Clark decide to build a winter fort at Mandan.

JUNE 13, 1805
Reach the Great Falls on the Missouri River.

AUGUST 18–29, 1805
Receive twenty-nine horses from Shoshone Indians for war axes, knives, and guns.

SEPTEMBER 12–22, 1805
Cross the Bitterroot Mountains on horseback.

OCTOBER 16, 1805
Reach the Columbia River.

NOVEMBER 7, 1805
Clark sights the Pacific Ocean.

JULY 3, 1806
Clark heads down the Yellowstone River while Lewis follows the Missouri River downstream.

AUGUST 12, 1806
The two parties reunite at the junction of the Yellowstone and Missouri Rivers.

Above **With the Louisiana Purchase, the United States acquired a territory larger than Britain, France, Germany, Italy, and Spain combined—at around four cents an acre. General Horatio Gates congratulated Jefferson, saying, "Let the land rejoice, for you have bought Louisiana for a song."**

SEPTEMBER 23, 1806
Lewis and Clark reach Saint Louis.

OCTOBER 1806
The two men are welcomed as heroes in Washington, DC.

OCTOBER 11, 1809
Lewis dies from self-inflicted wounds near Nashville, Tennessee.

1812
Sacagawea dies at Fort Manuel; Clark takes care of her two children.

SEPTEMBER 1, 1838
Clark dies in Saint Louis, aged 68.

The Louisiana Purchase

*I*n 1803, while Lewis and Clark were planning their journey, the news broke that the United States had made the Louisiana Purchase: President Jefferson had paid the French emperor Napoleon 60 million francs ($15 million) for a tract of land that stretched over 800,000 square miles (1.25 million km²), from Texas and Louisiana in the south to Montana and North Dakota in the north. Lewis and Clark would be the first to explore the new U.S. territories.

Lewis asked William Clark, an old comrade and friend from Caroline County, Virginia, to share command. It was a successful partnership, for both men were intelligent, resourceful military leaders who had experience of hardship in the wilderness.

Lewis and Clark Expedition route (1804–1806)

November 1805: Clark sights the Pacific Ocean; the expedition winters until March 1806.

July 1806: Lewis's party scuffles with Blackfeet.

June–July 1805: Lewis and Clark portage around the Great Falls of the Missouri.

October 1804–April 1805: Sacagawea joins expedition at Lewis and Clark's winter quarters.

May 14, 1804: Lewis and Clark leave Saint Louis.

Vancouver Island

Fort Clatsop

San Francisco

ROCKY MOUNTAINS

Bitterroot Mountains

Columbia

Marias

Milk

Great Falls

MONTANA

Yellowstone

NORTH DAKOTA

Fort Mandan

Black Hills

SOUTH DAKOTA

Bighorn Mountains

Snake

Bear Lake

Great Salt Lake

Green River

Sierra Nevada

Great Basin

Great American Desert

Mississippi

Des Moines

Missouri

Saint Louis

Arkansas

Mojave Desert

Lower California

Colorado

PACIFIC OCEAN

MEXICO

UNITED STATES OF AMERICA

Lake Winnipegosis

0   500 miles
0   800 km

Left **The Lewis and Clark expedition (1804–1806) laid the foundation for the extension of U.S. territory from the Atlantic to the Pacific.**

Lewis and Clark planned to follow the Missouri River to its source, cross the Rocky Mountains, and then track the Columbia River to where it emptied into the Pacific Ocean. On May 14, 1804, the expedition party, which numbered thirty-four, set out from Saint Louis, at the junction of the Missouri and Mississippi Rivers. For the first stretch of the voyage, the men used a specially designed fifty-five-foot (17 m) keelboat, which carried twelve tons (10,886 kg) of supplies. They also took two smaller and shallower draft vessels called pirogues. Rowing upstream and towing the boats when the current was too strong, the men struggled to cover ten miles a day. As winter set in, they built a small triangular fort north of present-day Bismarck, North Dakota,

and named it Mandan after the friendly local Indians.

In November 1804 Lewis and Clark met the French Canadian fur trapper Toussaint Charbonneau and hired him as an interpreter. Charbonneau was accompanied by one of his wives, a Shoshone Indian named Sacagawea. Though she was only sixteen and was carrying her infant son Jean-Baptiste on her back, Sacagawea helped guide the expedition through difficult country. She helped translate the Shoshone language and used her knowledge of local plants to tend the men when they were sick. The presence of Sacagawea in the party indicated that the corps came in peace, as women never traveled in war parties.

In April 1805 the Lewis and Clark expedition set off upstream once again. The spring meltwaters added great force to the river currents, and the men were forced on occasions to tow or push their boats and, around the Great Missouri Falls in present-day Montana, to carry them for long stretches. Other obstacles to their progress included attacks by bears and injuries from prickly pears, which pierced their feet through the soles of their boots. By August the party had reached the source of the Missouri River and crossed the Continental Divide. Lewis and Clark met with some Shoshone at Camp Fortunate. They traded weapons for horses and arranged for guides to lead them to the foot of the Bitterroot Mountains.

Below A 1906 photograph of Nez Percé Indians on horseback. Lewis and Clark exchanged gifts with the Nez Percé in 1805 and sheltered with them the following spring.

Encounters with American Indians

Lewis and Clark studied the customs and languages of the native inhabitants who lived in western North America. During the voyage, there were several dangerous encounters with the more warlike tribes. In September 1804 the Teton Sioux of South Dakota demanded one of the expedition's boats as tribute before they would allow the corps to pass farther up the river. In July 1806 a war party of Piegen Blackfeet warriors tried to steal the expedition's horses and guns. For the most part, however, the expedition members got on well with the tribes that they met. They awarded peace medals to the chiefs of the Ohio and Missouri nations and for five months traded successfully with the Mandan and Hidatsa who lived near Fort Mandan. Lewis described the helpful Nez Percé of the Bitterroot Mountains as "the most hospitable, honest, and sincere people that we have met."

As a result of the expedition, a delegation of important Sioux and Missouri chiefs traveled to Washington in 1806 to meet President Jefferson. Clark was trusted and befriended by many Indian leaders and in later life worked in public service as an Indian agent and as superintendent of Indian affairs.

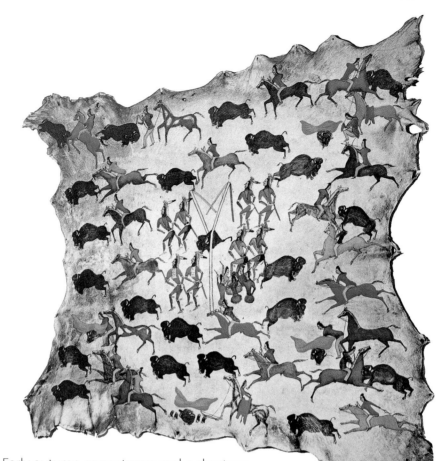

Early autumn snowstorms and a shortage of food severely endangered the expedition. Exhausted and on the point of starvation, the men were nursed back to health by the Nez Percé, who lived on the western slopes of the Rocky Mountains, in present-day north central Idaho.

In October 1805 the group built new canoes and set off down the Snake and Columbia Rivers, this time traveling with the current. In November they finally reached the Pacific coastline, 554 days and 4,132 miles (6,650 km) after leaving Saint Louis. On the return journey the party divided in two and explored the Yellowstone and Missouri river systems.

The Lewis and Clark expedition returned to Saint Louis in September 1806. Despite the dangers and hardship, only one member of the group had died. Lewis and Clark were hailed as national heroes when they visited Washington. Their achievement captured the imagination of the American public and helped fuel the American drive westward in the decades that followed.

Thomas Jefferson's instructions to Lewis demonstrated the importance the president placed on a sound knowledge of every aspect of Native American life:

. . . make yourself acquainted . . . with the names of the nations and their members . . . their language, traditions, monuments; their ordinary occupations in agriculture, fishing, hunting, war, arts, and the implements for these; their food, clothing, and domestic accommodations; the diseases prevalent among them, and the remedies they use . . . peculiarities in their laws, customs, and dispositions; and articles of commerce they may need.

Letter of commission to
Meriwether Lewis (1803)

SEE ALSO

- Mackenzie, Alexander • Native Peoples
- Sacagawea

LIVINGSTONE, DAVID

BORN IN SCOTLAND, DAVID LIVINGSTONE (1813–1873) achieved lasting fame for his work in Africa as a missionary and explorer. His journeys into uncharted regions of the African interior had two goals. The first was to spread Christianity; the second was to open up new trade routes, an endeavor he thought would bring about the end of the slave trade. As a result of Livingstone's three major expeditions, large parts of Africa were mapped for the first time.

FROM MILL WORKER TO MISSIONARY

David Livingstone was born into a poor family and lived with his mother, father, two brothers, and two sisters in a one-room apartment in the Scottish mill town of Blantyre, near Glasgow. In the early years of the nineteenth century, the Industrial Revolution—the transition from an economy based predominantly on agriculture to one based predominantly on industry—had led to the construction of a huge number of factories throughout Britain. These factories housed machines of mass production that menial workers were hired to operate. Many factories employed children, and by the age of ten, Livingstone was contributing to the family income by working fourteen-hour days at a Blantyre cotton mill.

After his day's work, David went to night school, where he proved a bright student. Raised a devout Christian, by the age of twenty, he had decided to devote his life to spreading the Christian faith in foreign lands.

In 1840 Livingstone qualified as a medical missionary. He joined the London Missionary Society and declared his desire to tend to the bodies and souls of people beyond the reach of Christianity. At first he wanted to work in China, but when war prevented his doing so, he was sent to Africa.

Right **David Livingstone as a young man.**

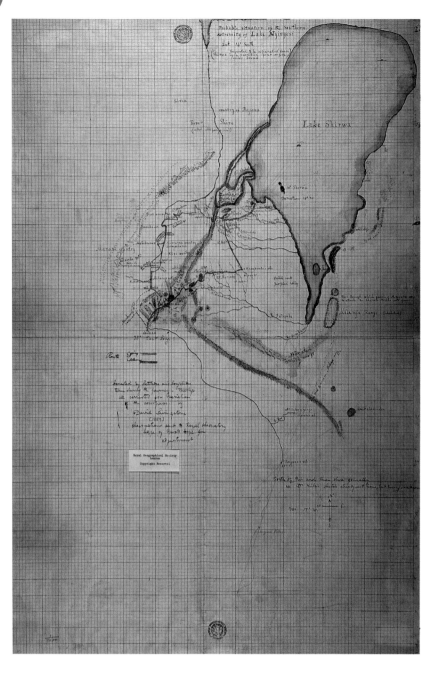

Above **This map of Lake Shirwa, in Malawi, was drawn by David Livingstone in 1859.**

EAGER TO EXPLORE

After a three-month boat trip from Britain, Livingstone arrived in southern Africa. He traveled by ox wagon seven hundred miles (1,100 km) north to Bechuanaland (present-day Botswana) and joined the mission at the village of Kuruman, on the southern edge of the Kalahari Desert.

Other missionaries worked in the immediate vicinity of the mission, but Livingstone was eager to spread Christianity farther afield. In 1844 he started a mission at Mabotsa, 250 miles (400 km) north of Kuruman. He was attacked by a lion there, and while recovering, he married Mary Moffat (1821–1862), the daughter of another missionary, Robert Moffat. In 1847 Livingstone set up a second mission, at Kolobeng, north of Mabotsa.

CROSSING THE KALAHARI

It was from Kolobeng that Livingstone began his first exploration of uncharted territory. In 1849 he and William Oswell headed north across the Kalahari Desert. They became the first Europeans to see Lake Ngami—a discovery that brought Livingstone to the attention of the Royal Geographical Society in London. The more Livingstone saw the effects of the slave trade on the peoples of the region, the more he vowed to work for its abolition. He thought that if routes could be opened up between the interior of Africa and the coast,

1813
Livingstone is born near Glasgow, Scotland.

1823
Begins work at a cotton mill.

1836
Begins to study medicine; plans to work as a Christian missionary in Africa.

1840
Qualifies as a doctor; joins the London Missionary Society and sails to southern Africa.

1849–1851
On three expeditions across the Kalahari Desert, discovers Lake Ngami and reaches the upper Zambezi River.

1853–1856
Makes the first crossing of Africa by a European; discovers the Victoria Falls.

1857
Publishes *Missionary Travels and Researches in Southern Africa*.

1858–1863
Attempts to navigate the Zambezi River.

1865
Publishes *Narrative of an Expedition on the Zambezi*.

1866–1871
Searches for the source of the Nile River and explores the area around Lakes Tanganyika, Mweru, and Bangweulu.

1871
Travels to the Lualaba River. Meets Henry Morton Stanley at Ujiji; the two men explore northern shore of Lake Tanganyika.

1873
Livingstone dies on the shore of Lake Bangweulu.

fair and equal trade would establish itself and would ultimately prove economically more viable than trade based on the enslavement of African peoples. Livingstone believed that Africa's rivers offered the best possibility of trade routes.

COAST TO COAST

Between November 1853 and May 1856, Livingstone led the first coast-to-coast crossing of Africa by Europeans, on which he covered some 4,300 miles (6,900 km). His trek took him first from Linyanti (in present-day Botswana) to the Portuguese port of Luanda (in Angola), on the Atlantic coast. On the way he contracted malaria and became weak, and his African porters threatened to turn back. Despite reaching the coast, Livingstone concluded that the route was not suitable for traders.

Livingstone the Missionary

David Livingstone's original purpose in Africa was to introduce Christianity to the indigenous people. In 1840 he joined the London Missionary Society, an organization founded in 1794 that sent missionaries around the world. During his early years in Africa, Livingstone set up several new missions. Yet although people traveled great distances to hear him preach and to have him tend to their ailments, he converted few Africans to Christianity. Livingstone's desire to explore the continent and search for viable trade routes brought him into conflict with the London Missionary Society. In 1858 he left the society in order to devote himself fully to exploration.

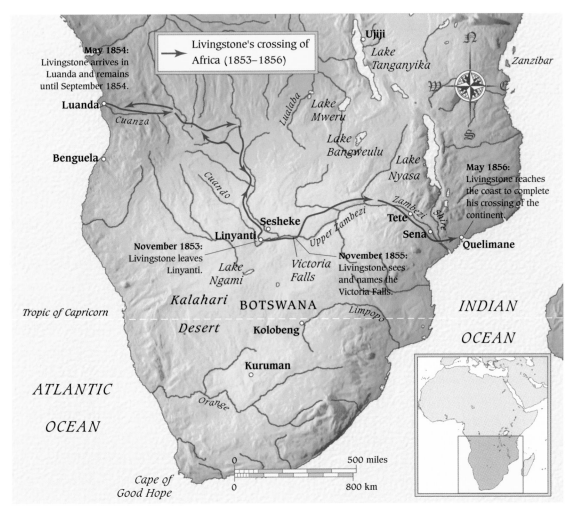

Left David Livingstone's travels took him far beyond the boundaries of charted territory.

May 1854: Livingstone arrives in Luanda and remains until September 1854.

Luanda

Benguela

Cuanza

Lualaba

Lake Mweru

Lake Bangweulu

Ujiji

Lake Tanganyika

Zanzibar

→ Livingstone's crossing of Africa (1853–1856)

Lake Nyasa

May 1856: Livingstone reaches the coast to complete his crossing of the continent.

Cuando

Sesheke

Linyanti

November 1853: Livingstone leaves Linyanti.

Lake Ngami

Victoria Falls

November 1855: Livingstone sees and names the Victoria Falls.

Upper Zambezi

Zambezi

Tete

Shire

Sena

Quelimane

Kalahari Desert

BOTSWANA

Limpopo

INDIAN OCEAN

Tropic of Capricorn

Kolobeng

Kuruman

ATLANTIC OCEAN

Orange

Cape of Good Hope

0   500 miles
0   800 km

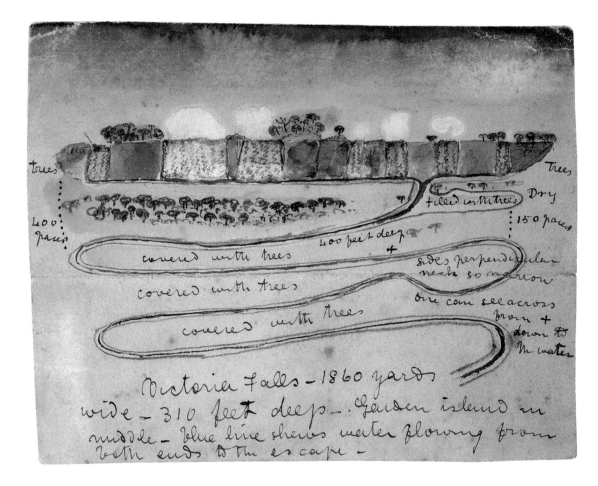

Having returned to Linyanti, Livingstone began a journey east along the Zambezi River. In November 1855 he came to huge waterfalls that, owing to the clouds of water vapor that hung around them and the deafening roar of the water, were known locally as Mosi Oa Tunya ("the smoke that thunders"). In honor of the Queen of England, Livingstone named them Victoria Falls. Continuing eastward, he completed his crossing of Africa when he reached Quelimane, on the Indian Ocean coast.

"GOD'S HIGHWAY"

When he returned to Britain in 1856, Livingstone was hailed as a national hero. He resigned from the London Missionary Society to become a full time explorer. In 1858 the British government provided funding for a five-year expedition to chart the Zambezi river system. For Livingstone the Zambezi was a means by which remote parts of Africa might be reached by traders and missionaries, and he referred to it for this reason as "God's highway." He gathered a wealth of data about central and eastern Africa and inadvertently encouraged European nations to begin their colonization of the region. The Zambezi expedition was difficult and dangerous, and many died, including Livingstone's wife.

Livingstone's first impressions of the Victoria Falls are captured in this excerpt:

. . . I believe that no one could perceive where the vast body of water went; it seemed to lose itself in the earth . . . creeping with awe to the verge, I peered down into a large rent which had been made from bank to bank of the broad Zambezi, and saw that a stream of a thousand yards broad leaped down a hundred feet, and then became suddenly compressed into a space of fifteen or twenty yards. The entire falls are simply a crack made in the hard basaltic rock . . . the most wonderful sight I had witnessed in Africa.

David Livingstone, *Missionary Travels and Researches in South Africa*

FINAL AFRICAN JOURNEY

In 1865 the Royal Geographical Society commissioned Livingstone to locate the source of the Nile River, which, despite the information provided by Richard Burton and John Hanning Speke in 1858, was greatly disputed.

Starting out at Zanzibar in 1866, Livingstone crossed to Lake Malawi (Lake Nyasa) and then onto Lake Tanganyika, known locally as the Sea of Ujiji. Despite food shortages and constant illness, Livingstone explored Lakes Mweru and Bangweulu and, in 1871, reached the Lualaba River, which he was convinced was a tributary of the Nile (but which later proved to be part of the Congo River).

When nothing was heard from Livingstone for three years, it was rumored that he was dead. The *New York Herald* newspaper sent Henry Morton Stanley to find Livingstone. Stanley's quest ended in one of the most famous meetings in history. Stanley entered the village of Ujiji, found the explorer ill and short of rations, and greeted him with the words, "Dr. Livingstone, I presume." Stanley helped Livingstone explore the northern end of Lake Tanganyika, which the men finally concluded was not a source of the Nile.

Stanley returned home, but Livingstone, determined to continue his exploration of the Lualaba, set off again in August 1872. Within six months he was dead from dysentery. Livingstone's African friends buried his heart under a tree and then carried his body on a five-month journey to the coast, from where it was shipped back to London for burial in Westminster Abbey.

SEE ALSO
- Burton, Richard Francis • Speke, John Hanning
- Stanley, Henry Morton

Below **This print, taken from an 1872 German woodcut, depicts Stanley's famous meeting with Livingstone at Ujiji on October 28, 1871.**

MACKENZIE, ALEXANDER

ALEXANDER MACKENZIE (1764–1820), A SCOTTISH FUR TRADER, was a pioneer in the exploration of North America. In 1789 he discovered and named the Mackenzie River and followed it to its mouth in the Arctic Ocean. Three years later Mackenzie became the first European to cross the North American continent; his journey helped to ensure that the territory of Canada extended west as far as the Pacific coast.

Above **This portrait of Alexander Mackenzie was painted by Thomas Lawrence around 1800.**

EARLY LIFE

Alexander Mackenzie was born in Stornoway on the Scottish island of Lewis in 1764. In 1774 his family emigrated to New York but moved on to Canada the following year when the American Revolution broke out. In 1779, at the age of fifteen, Alexander joined a Montreal fur-trading company, and eight years later he became a partner in the North West Company.

FIRST JOURNEY

From conversations with a veteran trader, Peter Pond, and from reports he had gathered while on fur-trading expeditions, Mackenzie concluded that a river passage connected the Great Slave Lake to the Pacific Ocean. To test his theory, he led a party of twelve people in three small birchbark canoes from Fort Chipewyan at the head of Lake Athabasca on June 3, 1789.

When Mackenzie and his companions reached the Great Slave Lake, they found it still frozen and were forced to camp out on the ice for six nights. They eventually crossed to the western end of the lake on June 29 and discovered the great river that now bears Mackenzie's name.

After a sixteen-day 1,100-mile (1,770 km) journey downstream, Mackenzie and his men reached the huge delta where the Mackenzie River enters the sea. Mackenzie, dismayed to find that the river flowed into the Arctic

Ocean and not into the Pacific, named it the River of Disappointment. Following a stay of four days on an island in the delta, his expedition returned safely to Fort Chipewyan on September 12.

IN SEARCH OF THE PACIFIC

Having discovered on his first journey that his measurements of latitude and longitude were inadequate, Mackenzie spent three years learning the latest surveying methods. In October 1792, still hoping to find a route across North America to the Pacific Ocean, he set off from Fort Chipewyan once more. This time he and his companions traveled southwest along the Peace River and wintered at Fort Fork. The expedition resumed in May 1793, once the snows had cleared, and made progress down the Fraser River.

Below **Every fall, native peoples brought furs, salt, and other goods to trading posts, such as Fort Resolution on the Great Slave Lake (photographed here in 1905).**

Voyageurs

There were many stages in the process that brought beaver furs from the Canadian interior to France. First, fur traders would explore the wilderness in search of groups of Indians. Next, they would persuade the Indians to enter an agreement to trap beavers, cure the skins, and bring the furs to a trading post to sell. Voyageurs were men engaged by fur traders to transport furs from those posts to the Saint Lawrence colony, from where they could finally be exported.

Traveling by canoe, the voyageurs paddled at a rate of forty strokes per minute for many hours at end. Speed was important, not only to bring the furs to market as quickly as possible but also to avoid being trapped in freezing rivers. The North West Company had over eleven hundred voyageurs, most of whom were French Canadians, natives from Quebec, and métis (those of mixed race). These men had to be fit, resourceful, and able to survive by living off the land.

HISLOP & NACLE

The Bella Coola, a tribe of Nuxalk Indians who lived along the north bank of the river they came to be named after, subsisted entirely on fish. Mackenzie discovered their abhorrence of meat when, having feasted on venison, he and his men tried to dispose of the bones:

These people indulge an extreme superstition respecting their fish, as it is apparently their only animal food. Flesh they never taste, and one of their dogs having picked and swallowed part of a bone which we had left, was beaten by his master till he disgorged it. One of my people also having thrown a bone of the deer in the river, a native, who had observed the circumstance, immediately dived and brought it up, and, having consigned it to the fire, instantly proceeded to wash his polluted hands.

The Journals and Letters of Sir Alexander Mackenzie

Mackenzie and his companions encountered several native peoples previously unknown to Europeans. While some were hostile, others were friendly, and one group warned Mackenzie about the dangerous rapids that lay in wait farther down the Fraser River. Heeding their advice, Mackenzie struck out overland instead. On June 21, 1793, Mackenzie finally reached the Pacific Ocean at the mouth of the Bella Coola River.

In late August the expedition returned safely to Fort Chipewyan. Mackenzie had traveled over 2,300 miles (3,833 km) and completed the first overland crossing of North America. Mackenzie's charts were the

Right **Driven by the desire to find a navigable passage across North America, Mackenzie reached the Arctic Ocean on his first journey and the Pacific on his second.**

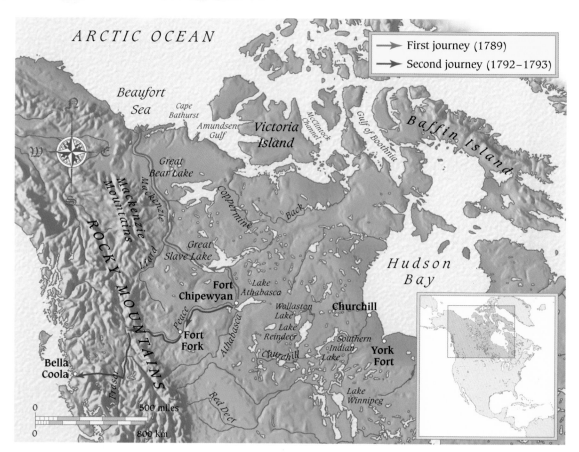

1764
Alexander Mackenzie is born on the Scottish island of Lewis.

1775
Mackenzie family moves to Canada.

1779
Mackenzie joins a fur-trading company.

1787
Becomes a partner in the North West Company.

JUNE 29, 1789
Discovers the Mackenzie River.

OCTOBER 1792
Begins second expedition to the west.

JUNE 21, 1793
Reaches the Pacific Ocean.

1801
Publishes account of his voyages.

1802
Is knighted by King George III.

1820
Dies in Perthshire, Scotland.

first accurate maps of the western Canadian river system, and his expedition had demonstrated the existence of a route to the Pacific across the Rocky Mountains. Yet the Rockies had scarce supplies of beaver, and the North West Company, concluding that the new route was unlikely to be profitable, made no plans to take advantage of Mackenzie's findings. In 1801 an account of his expeditions was published under the title *Voyages from Montreal through the Continent of North America to the Frozen and Pacific Oceans*.

LATER YEARS

Mackenzie's book was extremely popular, and he gained a degree of fame. In 1802 the English king, George III, knighted him. After three years as a member of the Lower Canada legislature, Mackenzie retired to his native Scotland a wealthy man. Although he never returned to western Canada, he urged the British crown to lay claim to the territories he had crossed. Thus, it was as a result of Mackenzie's exhortations that Canadian territory eventually stretched across the North American continent from the Atlantic to the Pacific. Mackenzie died in Perthshire in 1820. Eleven places and geographical features in British Columbia and the Northwest Territories, including a river, a bay, and a mountain range, still bear his name.

SEE ALSO

- La Vérendrye, Pierre Gaultier de Varennes de
- Lewis and Clark Expedition

Below **This portion of Mackenzie's own map of his travels shows the last stage of his journey westward, from the Rocky Mountains to the Pacific. The villages of the Bella Coola Indians are indicated on the lower reaches of the river that gives them their name.**

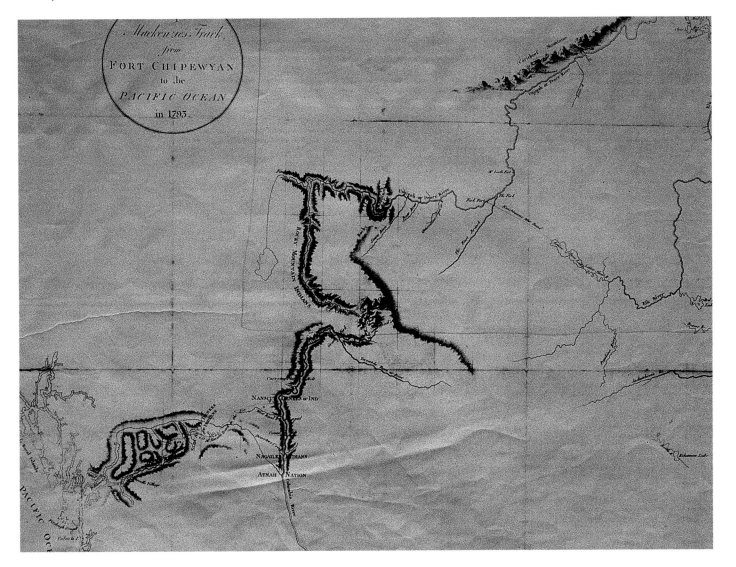

MAGELLAN, FERDINAND

THE PORTUGUESE EXPLORER FERDINAND MAGELLAN (c. 1480–1521) led the first expedition (1519–1522) to circumnavigate the globe (that is, to sail all the way around the world). Magellan's famous voyage revealed the vast size of the Pacific and demonstrated the extent to which earlier explorers, such as Christopher Columbus, had underestimated the difficulty of sailing west from Europe to Asia. The first circumnavigation revealed the world to be much larger than had previously been believed and proved once and for all that the world was round.

Below **In this sixteenth-century portrait, Magellan looks up at the stars. Astronomical observation was crucial to the completion of his voyage.**

EARLY LIFE

Ferdinand Magellan is the English form of the Portuguese name Fernão de Magalhães. Magellan was born around 1480 in northern Portugal. His parents died when he was still a boy, and he was brought up at the royal court. He served as a page until 1505, when he sailed to India as part of a Portuguese fleet under the command of Francisco de Almeida.

Magellan spent eight years serving as a soldier and sea captain and fought a series of campaigns against Portugal's Muslim rivals in the Indian Ocean. He also took part in a campaign in Morocco, where his wounds left him lame in one leg. After being wrongly accused of corruption, Magellan fell out of favor with King Manuel of Portugal. In 1514 the king refused Magellan's request for higher wages but gave him permission to look elsewhere for employment. In 1517 Magellan moved to Spain and presented himself at the court of King Charles I. His offer to lead a Spanish voyage of exploration to the Spice Islands of Southeast Asia was eagerly accepted.

IN SEARCH OF THE SPICE ISLANDS

In 1513 the Spanish explorer Vasco Núñez de Balboa had walked across America at its narrowest point (in present-day Panama). Just three weeks after leaving the Atlantic coast, he arrived at the Pacific Ocean (which he named the South Sea). His journey raised Magellan's hopes that there might exist a strait, or sea passage, through the American continent. If he were to discover such a strait, he reasoned, then the Spice Islands would lie only a short distance away.

Portugal and Spain

During the fifteenth and sixteenth centuries, Portugal and Spain were the two great rivals in world exploration. With the 1494 Treaty of Tordesillas, Pope Alexander VI divided the non-Christian world between them. A line was drawn at about 45 degrees west longitude, which ran about 1,110 miles (1,786 km) west of the Cape Verde Islands. Portugal could claim rights over any new discoveries that lay to the east of this line, while the west would belong to Spain.

The goal of both countries was to gain access to the spices of Asia. As the Portuguese now controlled the sea route to the east, the Spanish were forced to search for a route to Asia by sailing west. Yet Spanish voyages westward continually ran into one large obstacle: the Americas. Meanwhile, by 1512, the Portuguese had reached the Moluccas, the so-called Spice Islands of Southeast Asia, where the most expensive spices, such as cloves, grew. The Spanish, greatly underestimating the size of the Pacific Ocean, claimed that the Moluccas lay close to South America, and so, under the terms of the Treaty of Tordesillas, should belong to Spain rather than Portugal.

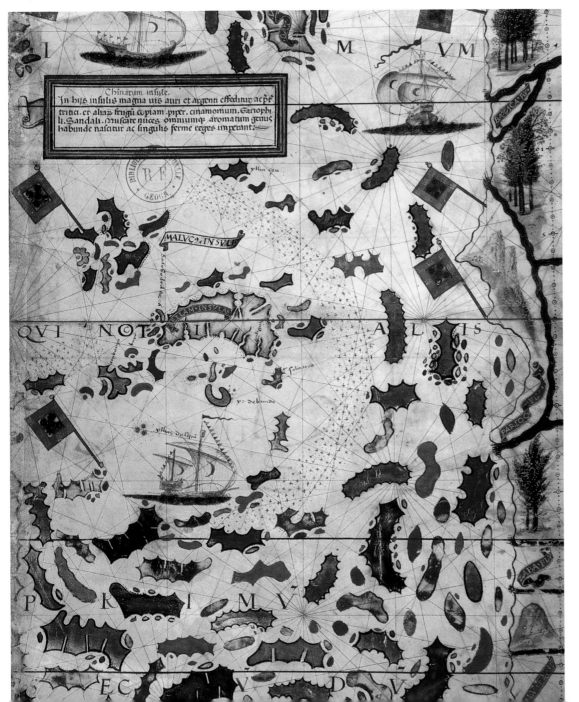

Left This Spanish map of the Spice Islands, published in 1519, is from an atlas of portolan charts. Portolan charts included lines indicating compass bearings and enabled a pilot to lay a course from harbor to harbor.

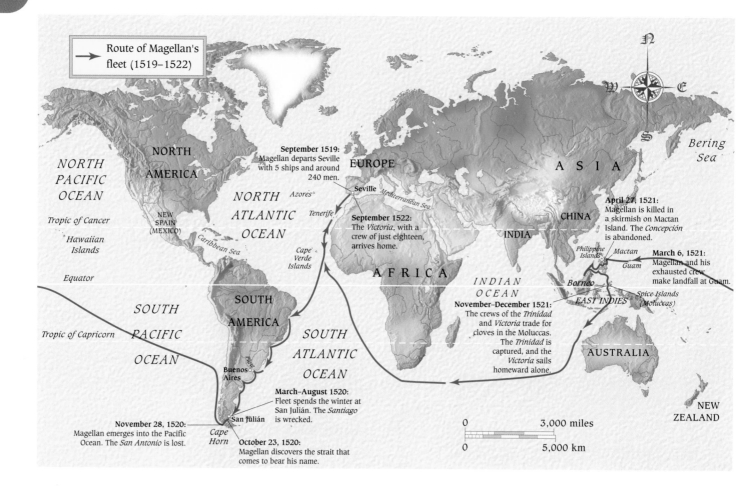

September 1519: Magellan departs Seville with 5 ships and around 240 men.

September 1522: The *Victoria*, with a crew of just eighteen, arrives home.

April 27, 1521: Magellan is killed in a skirmish on Mactan Island. The *Concepción* is abandoned.

March 6, 1521: Magellan and his exhausted crew make landfall at Guam.

November–December 1521: The crews of the *Trinidad* and *Victoria* trade for cloves in the Moluccas. The *Trinidad* is captured, and the *Victoria* sails homeward alone.

March–August 1520: Fleet spends the winter at San Julián. The *Santiago* is wrecked.

November 28, 1520: Magellan emerges into the Pacific Ocean. The *San Antonio* is lost.

October 23, 1520: Magellan discovers the strait that comes to bear his name.

0   3,000 miles
0   5,000 km

Above **Although he himself did not survive the epic voyage, Ferdinand Magellan is credited with leading the first-ever circumnavigation of the globe.**

THE FLEET SAILS

In September 1519 Magellan sailed toward South America from the southern Spanish port of Seville with a fleet of five ships: *Santiago, Concepción, San Antonio, Trinidad,* and *Victoria*. The company consisted of around 240 men; although most were Spaniards, the party also included thirty-seven Portuguese, thirty Italians, nineteen Frenchmen, one Englishman, and a German.

After crossing the Atlantic, Magellan began his search for a strait and by March 1520 had reached present-day southern Argentina. As the temperature dropped, Magellan set up winter quarters. On April 1, three Spanish captains, alarmed at the prospect of an icy winter in South America, staged a mutiny, which Magellan suppressed ruthlessly. One mutineer, Luis de Mendoza, was beheaded and chopped into four pieces. One part of his

---

1505
Magellan sails to India with Almeida.

1511
Takes part in the conquest of Malacca.

1513
Is wounded in Morocco.

1517
Moves to Spain.

MARCH 22, 1518
Receives royal backing for a westward voyage to the Indies.

SEPTEMBER 1519
Sails with five ships from Spain.

DECEMBER 1519
Reaches coast of South America.

MARCH 31, 1520
Reaches San Julián, where the fleet spends the next five months.

APRIL 1, 1520
Crushes a mutiny.

AUGUST 24, 1520
Sails again, heading south.

OCTOBER 21–NOVEMBER 28, 1520
Sails through the Strait of Magellan.

MARCH 16, 1521
Reaches the Philippines.

APRIL 27, 1521
Is killed in a battle on the island of Mactan.

NOVEMBER 1521
The *Trinidad* and *Victoria* reach the Moluccas, where the company trades for cloves.

SEPTEMBER 6, 1522
The *Victoria* returns to Spain.

An Italian who sailed with Magellan described the hellish Pacific crossing:

We ate biscuits, which were no longer biscuit, but powder of biscuits swarming with worms. . . . It stank strongly of the urine of rats. We drank yellow water that had been putrid for many days . . . and often we ate sawdust from boards. Rats were sold for one half ducado apiece, and even then we could not get them. But above all other misfortunes, the following was the worst. The gums of both the lower and the upper teeth of some of our men swelled, so that they could not eat under any circumstances and therefore died.

Antonio Pigafetta, *Magellan's Voyage*

quartered body, along with his head, was hung from a mast on each ship, as a warning against further rebellion. Soon after, the *Santiago* was wrecked.

With the arrival of spring, Magellan sailed south again. Finally, in October he discovered the mouth of the strait that came to bear his name. During an arduous thirty-eight-day journey through the Strait of Magellan, a second ship, the *San Antonio,* was lost when its crew deserted the expedition and sailed back to Spain.

CROSSING THE PACIFIC

On November 28 Magellan finally emerged from the strait into the open ocean, which he named the Pacific (peaceful), because its winds were so gentle. What Magellan did not know was that the Pacific is the world's largest ocean and covers a third of the earth's surface.

It took more than three months to sail across the Pacific, and by sheer bad luck Magellan missed all the many islands where he could have landed and taken on fresh water and food. As supplies ran low, his men began to starve to death or were stricken by scurvy, a disease caused by the lack of fresh food.

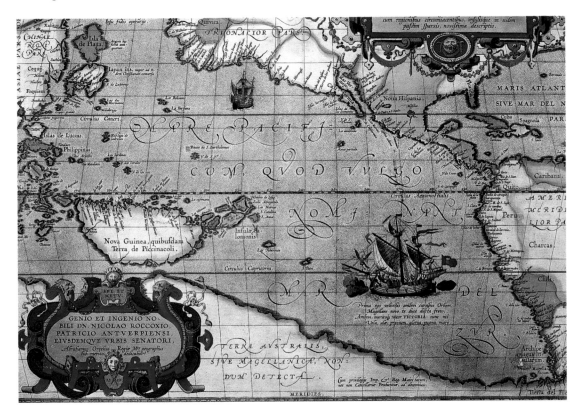

Left For a long time after Magellan's voyage, knowledge of the Pacific remained incomplete. On this 1589 map by the Dutch cartographer Abraham Ortelius, the size of the Pacific is greatly underestimated, and Magellan's ship is shown sailing to the north of a huge southern landmass (the speculative *Terra Australis*).

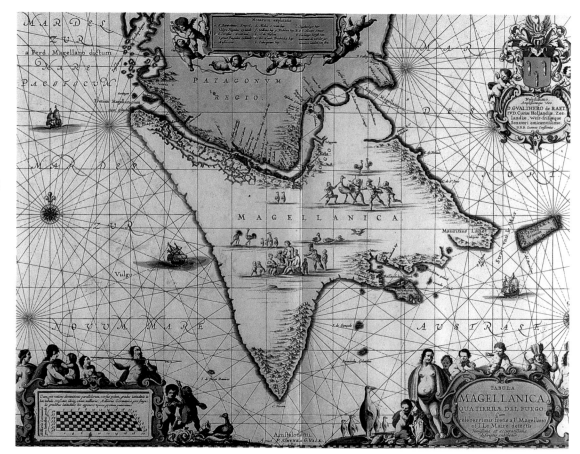

Magellan's death was witnessed by a member of his party:

The natives all hurled themselves upon him. One of them wounded him in the leg with a large cutlass. . . . That caused the captain to fall face downward, when immediately they rushed upon him with iron and bamboo spears and with their cutlasses, until they killed our mirror, our light, our comfort, and our true guide.

Antonio Pigafetta, *Magellan's Voyage*

LAND AT LAST

On March 6, 1521, the desperate men found the small island of Guam. When one of his ships' boats was stolen, Magellan captured and killed the thieves and burned down their village. A few days later, Magellan sailed on to the Philippines, which he claimed for Spain. On Mactan he offered to help a chief in a local war, and on April 27, 1521, fighting a battle in which he was vastly outnumbered, Magellan was killed along with several of his men.

THE LONG JOURNEY HOME

More disasters followed. A supposedly friendly king invited twenty-eight of the men to a feast and then had them all murdered. There being too few men to sail the three remaining ships, the *Concepción* was abandoned. The *Trinidad* was captured by the Portuguese.

Of the original fleet, only the *Victoria*, commanded by Juan Sebastián de Elcano, made it home to Spain and thus became the first ship to sail all the way around the world. Just eighteen men survived Magellan's voyage, all of them sick with scurvy. The *Victoria*'s cargo—twenty-four tons (21,772 kg) of cloves from the Moluccas—brought a good profit.

SEE ALSO

• Illness and Disease • Núñez de Balboa, Vasco

MAPMAKING

THE HISTORY OF MAPMAKING runs in close parallel to the history of exploration and discovery. Maps serve a dual function for explorers: before and during a journey they indicate the route or routes available, and after the journey they constitute a record of the route taken. Many journeys of discovery were launched with the simple purpose of traveling beyond the limits of what was known and of discovering and mapping new lands and seas. Maps provide a valuable historical insight into the gradually expanding dominion of humankind's knowledge of the world. By the end of the twentieth century, large areas of the earth were mapped in minute detail, and the attention of some mapmakers turned to charting the rest of the universe.

WHAT IS A MAP?

A map is a physical representation of a spatial area, generally (but not always) a part of the earth. Maps are drawn to scale—for example, on a map with a scale of 1:25,000, one inch on the map represents 25,000 inches on the ground.

The science (and art) of mapmaking is known as cartography. On a globe the earth may be represented as a sphere. Yet navigators require a flat surface on which to plot a course with mathematical accuracy. Thus, a great problem for cartographers is how to project the curved surface of the earth onto the flat surface of a map (a technique known as map projection).

MAPS IN THE ANCIENT WORLD

The earliest surviving maps date from around 2300 BCE. Archaeologists have found ancient maps, showing local land boundaries, inscribed on clay tablets by people living in Babylonia (present-day southern Iraq) and on the walls of Egyptian tombs.

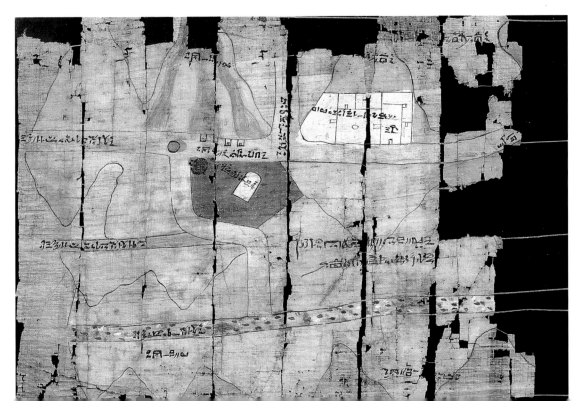

Left **This map, one of the oldest ever found, was made by Egyptian mapmakers around 1150 BCE. It shows the gold mines of Wadi Hammamat, an area of the Sinai Mountains in the Eastern Desert.**

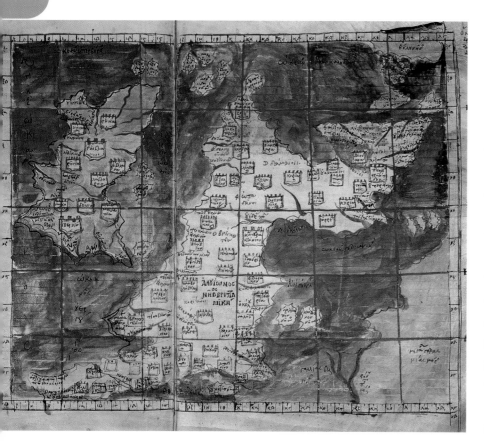

lines of latitude and longitude to pinpoint the precise location of geographical features also originated in ancient Greece.

For the ancient Romans, maps were useful tools in the efficient running of the empire. Roman maps provided important information for military campaigns, agreements on territories and boundaries, and navigation. Very few examples have survived; the nature of Roman maps can only be guessed at from descriptions of them.

The most important ancient mapmaker was Ptolemy (90–168 CE), whose *Geography* contained the earliest information about the African and Asian coasts of the Indian Ocean, principles for map projection, and a list of around eight thousand place names with their latitude and longitude.

MEDIEVAL MAPS

On maps of the early Middle Ages (a period that lasted from around 500 to 1000), the three known continents, Europe, Asia, and Africa, were separated by a T formed by the Nile River and Mediterranean Sea. The land was surrounded on all sides by a circular ocean, and so such maps are referred to as T and O renderings. In the late twelfth century, knowledge of the magnetic compass came to Europe from China, where it had been invented, and the first nautical charts emerged shortly afterward.

Above **Although none of Ptolemy's own maps survive, they were copied by medieval scholars. This map of the British Isles is from a twelfth- or thirteenth-century manuscript found in a monastery in Greece.**

The Greeks were the outstanding mapmakers of the ancient world. As the area of the world under Greek control grew, so did the area covered by Greek maps. The historian Herodotus traveled widely around 500 BCE and drew the first recognizable maps of Europe and Africa. The theory that the world is a sphere originated with the Greek mathematician Pythagoras in the sixth century BCE and was proved two hundred years later by the philosopher Aristotle. The idea of using

c. 2300 BCE
The earliest surviving maps are drawn in Mesopotamia and Egypt.

c. 350 BCE
The Greek philosopher Aristotle proves that the earth is a sphere.

c. 150 CE
Ptolemy completes his *Guide to Geography.*

1154
The Arab geographer al-Idrisi produces his world map.

1300
The Hereford *mappa mundi* is produced.

1507
Waldseemüller's world map, one of the first printed maps to include the New World discoveries, is produced.

1508
The Florentine cartographer Francesco Rosselli draws the first map of the entire globe, although ocean areas are too small and a mythical southern continent is included.

1569
The first Mercator projection world map is produced.

1917
Aerial photography is used for the first time as an aid to mapmakers.

1968
The first pictures of the earth from space are seen live on television.

1970
GIS (Geographic Information System) is designed, and high-speed digital computers are used to assimilate geographical data.

THE AGE OF DISCOVERY

A combination of factors in the late fifteenth century resulted in spectacular advances in mapmaking. The works of Ptolemy were rediscovered, and innovations in navigation, ship design, and astronomical observation coincided with the invention of printing. As Columbus made the first Asia-bound journeys westward in the 1490s, accurate maps were being mass-produced for the first time.

During the fifteenth and sixteenth centuries, many of the world's leading mapmakers were Dutch. The foremost of them, Gerardus Mercator (1512–1594), devised a means of map projection that is still in use.

Abraham Ortelius (1527–1598) produced the first modern atlas, *Theatrum orbis terrarum*. It was in Portugal, however, that Martin Behaim (1459–1507), a German navigator and explorer, made the first globe.

The English humorist Jonathan Swift (1667–1745) lived in an age when much of the African interior remained unmapped:

So geographers, in Afric maps,
With savage pictures fill their gaps,
And o'er unhabitable downs
Place elephants for want of towns.

Jonathan Swift, *On Poetry*

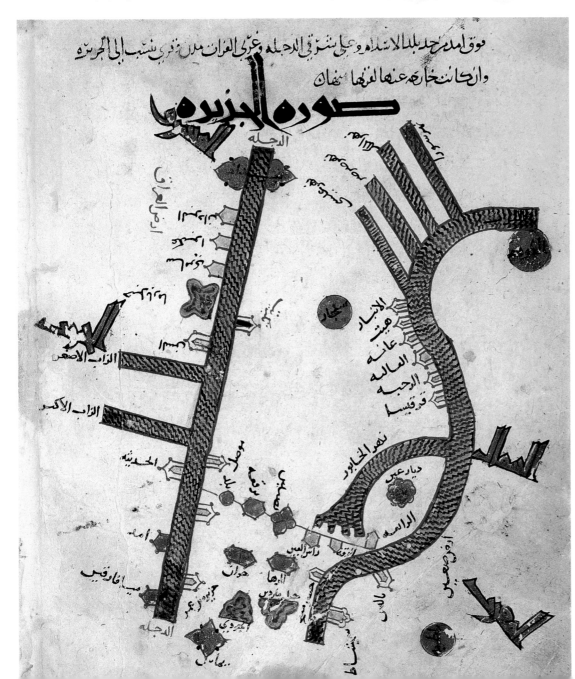

Left **This map of the Tigris and Euphrates Rivers (in present-day Iraq) is part of an atlas produced by the Arab geographer al-Istakhri in the tenth century.**

BUILDING A MAP OF THE WORLD

By the middle of the eighteenth century, geographers were constructing world maps roughly correct in outline except for three areas: the northwest coast of America, the northeast coast of Asia, and Antarctica. The first two areas were mapped by the British explorer Captain James Cook (1728–1779); the coast of Antarctica was first sighted and mapped by Charles Wilkes (1798–1877), a U.S. navy captain. Other British voyages led to accurate mapping of Burma and India. Christian missionaries gathered valuable cartographical data from remote regions of China and South America. The outline of Europe was well mapped by 1800, and attention turned to more detailed surveys of the interior. However, in North America, the lack of proper maps prompted George Washington to complain in 1775 that for geographical information he had to make do with "sketches and rumors."

PICTURING THE WORLD

Until the Age of Discovery, the majority of humankind had no knowledge of the world as a whole. During the Middle Ages, world maps were less a picture of the world than a picture of how the world was imagined to be. Christian maps, such as the Hereford *mappa mundi* (map of the world), place Jerusalem at the center and Paradise at the top, closer to

Right **The largest and most elaborate medieval map in existence, the *mappa mundi* (c. 1300), housed in Hereford Cathedral in western England, is decorated with around five hundred drawings of the history of humankind, as it was envisioned in the medieval church.**

Left The representation of a hill in the shape of an elephant on this 1923 map is extremely well executed and, unsurprisingly, remained undetected for some time.

God. Figures of Adam and Eve and of the Apostles are often included. Muslim maps placed Mecca, the birthplace of Mohammed, at the center of the earth. Ancient Indian maps have the mythical Mount Meru as the *axis mundi*, or center of the world.

Many maps are not only representations of the world but also works of art. Throughout the history of cartography, areas lacking detail on maps—large oceans or uncharted lands, for instance—have been filled with a range of pictures and designs. Examples include fantastical monsters and savages living in unexplored Africa, blowing faces representing the winds, a coat of arms belonging to the mapmaker's patron, and, in a map of 1550 by the French mapmaker Pierre Desceliers, pictures of legendary battles in northwestern America between pygmies and cranes.

HIDDEN HUMOR

The more mundane aspects of a mapmaker's work—the meticulous plotting of hills and valleys, currents and tides, and coastlines—can be arduous. On occasion bored mapmakers have livened up their work. One group of British soldiers, surveying a remote part of West Africa in 1923, had one hill left to record at the end of a long hot day. Perhaps to get the job done quickly or perhaps as a joke among themselves, they drew the hill in the shape of an elephant.

In 1903 a reluctant British mapmaker was ordered by one Captain Corry to map the Greek island of Lemnos. He labeled a row of four hills near the port Yam, Yrroc, Eb, and Denmad, names that were unknown locally. It was not until the 1920s that someone noticed that the names written backward spelled "May Corry Be Damned."

Martin Waldseemüller *c. 1470–c. 1518*

*A*t first it was generally believed that the lands Columbus had discovered in 1492 were part of Asia. In 1507 Martin Waldseemüller, a German geographer, produced the first printed map to depict these lands as a separate continent—a New World, separated from Asia by an ocean. The full title of Waldseemüller's work was *A Map of the Whole World according to the Teaching of Ptolemy and of Amerigo Vespucci and of Other Surveyors.* Waldseemüller had been so impressed by the voyages of Vespucci that he named the New World America.

Names and Claims

For imperial powers seeking to expand their territory overseas, mapping a place for the first time amounted to a claim of ownership. In 1616 the English explorer John Smith named a part of North America New England. He then drew up maps on which Indian names were replaced by English substitutes. (Anmoughcawgen, for instance, became Cambridge.) While Smith did not forcibly remove the native peoples, he certainly committed an act of symbolic dispossession.

The View from on High

During the twentieth century, sophisticated photographic equipment, carried aloft in hot air balloons and airplanes, enabled cartographers to map the earth's surface with remarkable accuracy. During World War I (1914–1918) aerial photography was an important aid to military planning, and during World War II (1939–1945) it was used to map large parts of North Africa and Asia. By the end of the twentieth century, the only part of the earth's surface that had not been mapped in great detail was the largely frozen continent of Antarctica.

SEE ALSO

- Geography • Idrisi, al-Sharif al-
- Latitude and Longitude • Map Projection
- Mercator, Gerardus • Navigation • Ptolemy
- Remote Sensing

Below **This infrared image of Charleston, South Carolina, was taken by *Landsat* in 1982. Active vegetation appears red and pink, water bodies are black, and urban structures appear in shades of white to light blue.**

The Earth from Space

When the first pictures were beamed back from the 1968 *Apollo 8* mission and broadcast around the world via live television, the effect was profound. As the twentieth century drew to its close, dozens of low-altitude satellites were orbiting the earth many times a day, gathering information that explorers and cartographers once labored hundred of years to provide. Remote-sensing technologies and high-speed digital computers enabled intricate mapping not only of the shape of the earth's surface but also of any number of geographical, geological, and geopolitical features, such as land use, the ocean floor, layers beneath the polar ice caps, population densities, and holes in the ozone layer.

MAP PROJECTION

THE FACT THAT THE EARTH IS A SPHERE and that maps are generally flat has presented mapmakers throughout history with a great mathematical problem. Map projection, the attempt at a solution to the problem, is the science of projecting the curved, three-dimensional surface of the earth onto a flat, two-dimensional plane. Cartographers have approached the problem in a number of ways, and the results are surprisingly varied.

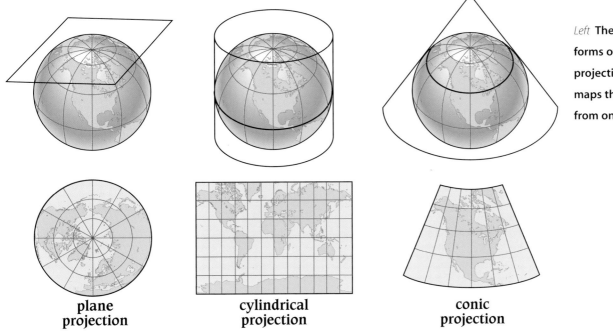

Left **The three basic forms of map projection produce maps that differ greatly from one another.**

plane projection	**cylindrical projection**	**conic projection**

Map projection became a serious concern during the fifteenth and sixteenth centuries, when, for the first time, there was a real possibility of accurately mapping large sections of the earth's surface. Accurately projected maps were essential if seafaring explorers traveling across thousands of miles of open ocean were to be able to locate themselves and plot their courses.

TYPES OF PROJECTION

The central mathematical problem is that a sphere cannot be transformed into a plane without some distortion, such as stretching, shrinking, or tearing. The process is akin to taking the peel of an orange and trying to flatten it onto a table. Several geometrical properties are involved: scale, angles, areas, distances, and directions. As a given projection cannot preserve all of these properties, one or more are sacrificed.

PLANE PROJECTIONS

On the simplest form of projection, a plane (flat surface) is imagined to touch the surface of the earth at a given point. Rays are imagined to emanate from another given point. The rays pass across the surface of the earth and onto the plane. The point at which a ray touches the earth will then be projected onto the plane at the point where the ray ends up. The result is a circular map. Plane projections cover only portions of the earth's surface—at most a hemisphere.

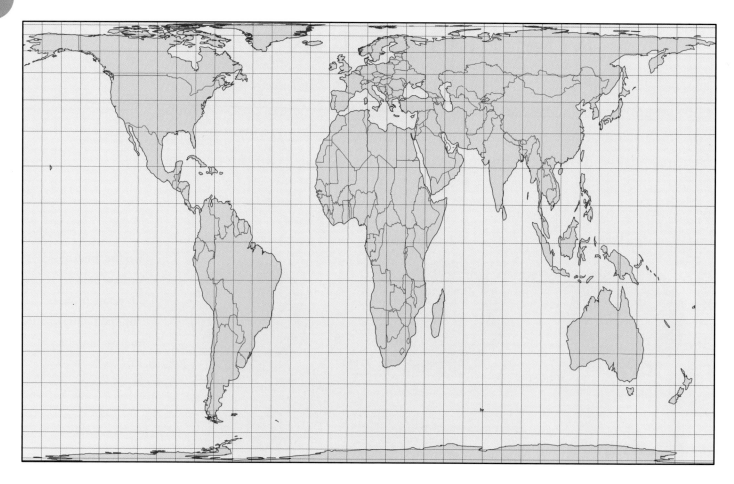

On gnomonic projections, the imaginary rays emanate from the center of the earth. As a result, any so-called great circle—the shortest possible path from one point on the earth to another—is represented as a straight line. This projection is therefore of great aid to navigators. The first use of the gnomonic projection was on the star map drawn by the ancient Greek astronomer Thales of Miletus in the sixth century BCE.

CYLINDRICAL PROJECTIONS

The most effective projection involves, in effect, wrapping the earth in a cylinder, projecting the image onto the inside of the cylinder, and then "unrolling" the cylinder. First devised and produced by the Dutch cartographer Gerardus Mercator in 1569, this projection is widely used on navigation charts. Any straight line on a map projected cylindrically is a "straight line" in the world; thus, a sailor or pilot can plot a course simply

by drawing a line between two points on a Mercator map, placing a compass on the map, and following the appropriate bearing. In the 1970s, four hundred years after it first emerged, Mercator's projection was the basis of the space oblique Mercator (SOM) projection, used to translate photographs of the earth taken from space into maps.

Above **The Peters projection offers a view of the world that differs considerably from that provided by the more familiar Mercator projection.**

The Peters Projection

*I*n 1973 a German scientist, Dr. Arno Peters, argued that the world's poorer countries, many of which are gathered around the equator, are represented unfairly on a Mercator map. He devised a new cylindrical projection, the Peters equal-area projection, that preserved the size of landmasses but greatly distorted their shape. As on Mercator's map, meridians are horizontal and parallels are vertical. Thus, any two points can be seen in their precise relationship in terms of distance and direction. A comparison of the Peters and Mercator projections clearly demonstrates that all map projections involve distortion of some kind.

MERCATOR'S DISTORTIONS

Mercator's map is a conformal projection, that is, one on which the shapes of landmasses are rendered accurately. All projections involve one form of compromise or another; on a Mercator map, the sizes of landmasses are distorted, particularly toward the Poles. On a Mercator projection, Greenland, for example, appears to be roughly equal in size to Africa. In reality, Africa is fourteen times larger than Greenland.

OTHER PROJECTIONS

For conic projections, a cone is imagined to be placed over the earth, touching it at all points on a given parallel. The map is projected onto the inside of the cone, and the cone is then slit and laid out flat. The Lambert conformal conic projection (1772) imagines the cone to cut through the surface of the earth, intersecting it at two parallels. Polyconic projection assumes a series of cones touch the globe, and the resulting map is a combination of all those results.

On pseudocylindrical projections, parallels are straight and equally spaced. The central meridian (the equator) is straight, but other meridians curve increasingly the farther they are from the equator (a characteristic that gives the map a more rounded appearance). The result is a compromise view of the world, with all geometrical properties distorted equally moderately. The best-known examples of this technique are the Van der Grinten projection (1904) and the Robinson projection (1960). The Winkel Tripel projection (1921) is currently endorsed by the National Geographic Society, and the Eckert projection (1906) is also widely used.

In the twentieth century, new world maps were drawn up not by projection in the purest form but by a process of mathematical plotting, using complex trigonometry. The best-known example is the interrupted homolosine projection of J. Paul Goode, an American cartographer. Toward the end of the century, map projections were generally performed by computers.

SEE ALSO

• Mapmaking • Mercator, Gerardus

Below **J. Paul Goode created this interrupted homolosine projection in 1923. The interruptions distort the oceans in order to preserve the geometrical properties of the continents (another version, interrupted to preserve the unity of the oceans, greatly distorted the continents).**

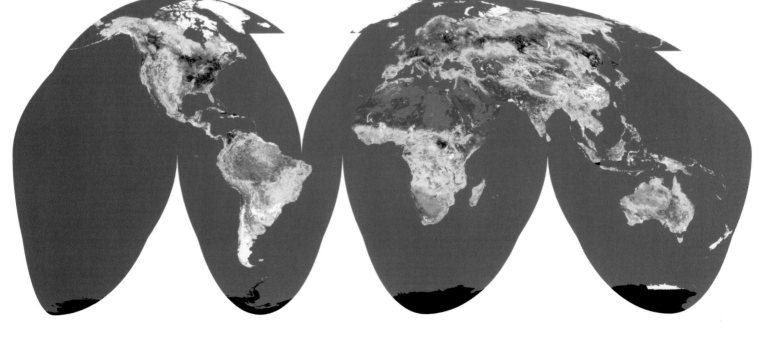

MARQUETTE, JACQUES

BORN IN 1637, the French Jesuit missionary Jacques Marquette joined the French Canadian explorer Louis Jolliet on an expedition (1673) that explored much of the Mississippi River. Marquette produced a very accurate map and a highly descriptive account of their trip before he died in 1675.

Below **This statue of Marquette stands in Milwaukee, Wisconsin, a city that also has a university named for the Jesuit explorer.**

YOUTH AND TRAINING

Jacques Marquette had a quick mind and a deep interest in religion and by the age of nine was being taught at a college run by Jesuits (a Roman Catholic order). At seventeen he decided to become a Jesuit himself and intensified his studies. His cherished ambition was to go to New France, the French colony in North America, and convert Native Americans to Christianity.

MISSIONARY LIFE

In 1666 Marquette was ordained as a priest and sent to New France. After learning some Native American languages, he was sent to the Great Lakes. Late in 1669 he reached the mission of La Pointe du Saint-Esprit, on the southern shore of Lake Superior. He stayed there for eighteen months until conflict with the Sioux forced him to leave. He and his Native American charges settled on the northern shore of the Straits of Mackinac, a narrow body of water that connects Lakes Michigan and Huron and separates the two peninsulas of Michigan. There Marquette set up a new mission, Saint Ignace.

1637
Jacques Marquette is born in Laon, France.

1654
Decides to become a Jesuit.

1656
Begins to study philosophy.

1666
Is sent by the Jesuits to New France.

1668
Begins work at mission of La Pointe du Saint-Esprit.

1671
Founds mission of Saint Ignace at Mackinac.

1673
Explores Mississippi River with Louis Jolliet.

1674
Attempts to establish a mission among Illinois River people.

1675
Dies at the mouth of the Père Marquette River, on the eastern shore of Lake Michigan.

A COMMISSION

In 1672 Louis Jolliet arrived at Saint Ignace. He was preparing an expedition to find the Mississippi River, which the French knew about from Native American accounts, and to discover whether it emptied into the Gulf of Mexico or the Pacific Ocean. Jolliet had orders from the Jesuits instructing Marquette to join the journey.

THE VOYAGE

In the middle of May 1673, the ice that had been blocking the Straits of Mackinac finally thawed. Jolliet, Marquette, and five others set out "fully resolved," Marquette wrote, "to do and suffer everything for so glorious an undertaking."

The party moved along northern Lake Michigan and up Green Bay, where the men entered the Fox River. Ignoring warnings of "horrible monsters which devoured men and canoes together," they portaged from the Fox to the Wisconsin River. This river brought them to the Mississippi, which they entered "with a joy," Marquette wrote, "that I cannot express."

The explorers passed the points where the Ohio and Missouri Rivers enter the Mississippi. When they reached the Missouri, they named it the Muddy River because it carried dirt and debris into the Mississippi at a powerful rate. They wondered if this river might lead as far as California.

The Jesuits in New France

The Jesuits played an important role in the development of New France. In 1632 the French government gave them control over all missionary work in large areas of the colony. The Jesuits used this right to travel throughout the region and attempt to convert Native Americans. As a result, good relations developed between the French and several Native American groups. The Jesuits' travels also extended French knowledge of the rivers and lakes of the region.

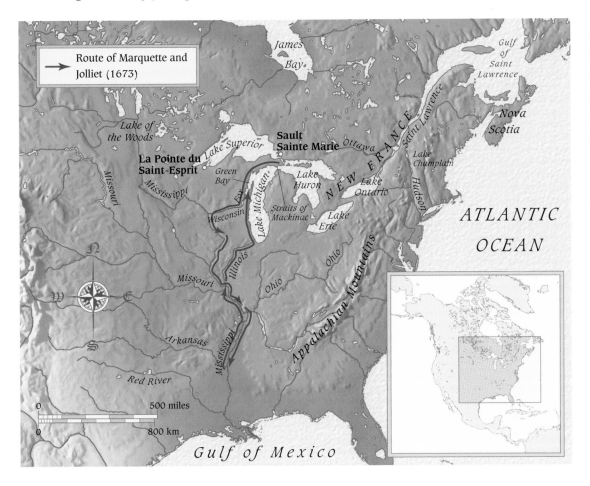

Left **Jolliet and Marquette traveled to within approximately four hundred miles (644 km) of the mouth of the Mississippi. Their trip confirmed that the river flowed into the Gulf of Mexico.**

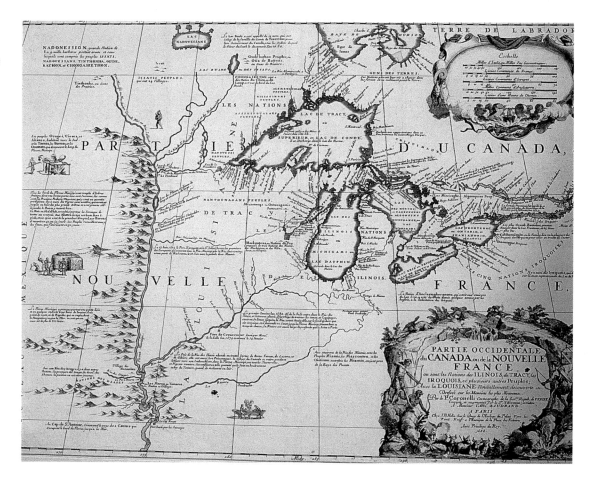

A month after entering the Mississippi, Marquette and Jolliet were told by a guide that they were about ten days' journey from the Mississippi's mouth. Convinced that the river flowed to the Gulf of Mexico and worried that they might be captured by Spanish forces, the explorers decided to return. They turned off the Mississippi into the Illinois River, portaged near present-day Chicago, and continued along the western shore of Lake Michigan, where they rested at the Jesuit mission of Saint Francis Xavier, in Green Bay.

FINAL YEARS

The rigors of the journey had made Marquette ill. He stayed at the mission for a year, and in late 1674, determined to continue his missionary work, he returned to the people along the Illinois River. In early 1675, when his health did not improve, he decided to return to Saint Ignace. He died on the way, on the eastern shore of Lake Michigan.

For the Jesuit record of events in New France, Marquette described the bison he and Jolliet saw grazing near a river in 1672:

The head is very large; the forehead is flat and a foot and a half wide between the horns, which are exactly like those of our oxen. . . . On the back is a rather high hump. . . . The flesh and the fat are excellent, and constitute the best dish at feasts. Moreover they are very fierce. . . . When attacked, they catch a man on their horns, if they can, toss him in the air, and then throw him on the ground, after which they trample him under foot, and kill him.

Father Claude Dablon, *Relation*

SEE ALSO

- Champlain, Samuel de • Jolliet, Louis
- La Salle, René-Robert Cavelier de

MERCANTILISM

MERCANTILISM WAS THE NAME LATER GIVEN to the economic practices pursued by the main European powers, especially in relation to their overseas colonies, from the sixteenth to the eighteenth centuries. Mercantilist governments exercised rigorous control of their national economy and attempted to direct the movement of all wealth within their own borders and to keep it there. Mercantilist powers passed laws that greatly favored their own merchants and farmers and virtually excluded rival foreign traders from any involvement in their economy by means of punitive taxes. The theory and practice of mercantilism lost much of their appeal in the nineteenth century as Great Britain and other free-trading nations grew very wealthy.

Below **Mercantilism brought about much conflict in Europe. In 1738 a British sailor, Captain Robert Jenkins, alleged that Spanish coast guards had boarded his ship in the Caribbean and cut off his ear—the ensuing War of Jenkins's Ear lasted three years.**

MERCANTILISM IN THE SPANISH EMPIRE

In the sixteenth century Spain became the first great mercantilist economy, largely because the conquests of explorers such as Hernán Cortés and Francisco Pizarro had won a large empire whose overseas territories were rich in precious metals. A key mercantilist belief was that the wealth of a nation was based on the amount of precious metal, especially gold and silver, that it owned.

Above **Queen Elizabeth's profit from Francis Drake's 1577 raid on the Spanish colonies paid the entire English debt.**

The Spanish crown carefully controlled the valuable resources of its colonies in the New World. Gold and silver bullion, the treasure of the Aztecs and Incas, was transported to Spain in heavily defended galleons. Landed estates in Spanish America were entrusted only to noble Spanish-born lords called *peninsulares*. The lucrative trade in slaves, who were taken from Africa to the plantations of present-day Cuba, Haiti, and Puerto Rico, was

1540
The Spanish crown uses the *asiento* contract system to control the transatlantic slave trade.

c. 1560
English privateers attack Spanish bullion fleets.

1620
English Parliament bans tobacco imported from Spanish and Dutch colonies in America.

1651
English Navigation Acts are passed by Parliament under Oliver Cromwell.

1665–1683
Jean-Baptiste Colbert, a mercantilist, rules as chief minister of France.

1765
The Spanish begin to open up their ports to foreign traders.

1776
The Scottish economist Adam Smith publishes the *Wealth of Nations*.

1789
The Spanish crown abolishes the failing *asiento* system.

1815
Free-trading Great Britain dominates world trade and industry.

also strictly controlled by the Spanish crown. The king granted private merchants an *asiento* (contract) that gave them exclusive trading rights for a period of seven to ten years. This arrangement made it easy for the crown to raise taxes on slave cargoes.

Until 1720 Spanish merchant ships from the colonies were permitted to unload their cargo only at the port of Seville. To protect craftsmen and manufacturers in Spain, the colonists were allowed to produce only a limited range of goods. Farmers in the colonies were forbidden from planting crops that grew in Spain, such as olives and grapes. The Spanish monarchy did everything to channel the empire's wealth toward the center and to make sure that merchants from foreign powers, such as England, could not trade on Spanish territory.

ENGLISH MERCANTILISM

Queen Elizabeth I of England (reigned 1558–1603) also followed mercantilist policies. She awarded licenses to privateers, professional pirates who harried the Spanish treasure fleets and tried to plunder the Spanish trade routes in America. Elizabeth encouraged privateering because she needed her share of the treasure to pay for war against Spain. As a mercantilist, she also believed that there was only a limited amount of wealth in the world. She reasoned that if English ships captured Spanish bullion, her enemy's treasure chest would be severely depleted and thus she would have a double advantage.

MERCANTILISM AND THE NATION-STATE

Mercantilism was an important force in the growth of European nation-states such as France and Spain. For long periods between 1500 and 1800, the nations of Europe were either at war with one another or preparing for war with one another. Mercantilism helped

The Navigation Acts

A series of laws known as the Navigation Acts was passed by the English Parliament from as early as 1381; they were effective chiefly in the seventeenth and eighteenth centuries. The Navigation Acts were intended to ensure that Britain's colonies in the Americas traded only with British merchants. Only British ships, manned by British crews, were allowed to trade in American ports. A list was drawn up of certain "enumerated" American commodities that had to be shipped to Britain before they could be sold to other countries in Europe. Under this rule British merchants could buy American raw materials, such as tobacco and cotton, cheaply and then turn them into more valuable finished products in British factories. It also made it easy for the British government to raise taxes on these materials. The Navigation Acts succeeded in squeezing Dutch and French merchants out of British America. They also helped colonial industries, which were protected from foreign competition and supported by subsidies from the government in London. Shipbuilding in New England prospered under this mercantilist system, while the Carolinas were given monopolies on key goods such as indigo, pitch, turpentine, and timber.

the developing states to organize their resources—such as population, food, and money. A mercantilist ideology also encouraged national governments to establish overseas colonies. Colonies not only were an important source of cheap materials but might also develop into overseas empires that would add to the power, influence, and illustriousness of the mother country.

Right **The Scottish economist Adam Smith believed that mercantilist ideas were wrong and that prosperity depended upon being able to trade as freely as possible.**

THE DECLINE OF MERCANTILISM

Mercantilist ideas enjoyed only partial success. The economy of France, for example, under the mercantilist policies of Jean-Baptiste Colbert (1619–1683), prospered at first. However, Louis XIV used the resources that Colbert had built up to fund a series of ruinous wars around the globe. Farmers in France resented the high taxes that they had to pay. The price of food rose, and general discontent among the population festered. (This general discontent was one of the causes of the social upheavals of the French Revolution in 1789). In Spain the import of American bullion led to steep inflation. Before long, rather than leading Europe, mercantilist Spain began to lag behind the other nations.

In Britain, until 1763 the mercantilist Navigation Acts were not enforced strongly, and there was a great deal of smuggling between British America and Europe. After 1763, however, the British government wanted the colonies to pay their share of the cost of the expensive wars against France. In seeking to apply the Navigation Acts and other tax laws more stringently, the British government provoked a deep resentment in colonial America. This resentment escalated into protests that eventually led in the 1770s to the American War of Independence.

Jean-Baptiste Colbert *1619–1683*

*A*ppointed finance minister of France in 1665, Jean-Baptiste Colbert believed that in order to become the most powerful nation in Europe, France would need not only a strong army and navy but also a strong economy. To realize this ambition and to build up France's overseas trade and maritime power, he pursued mercantilist policies. He especially encouraged shipbuilding, so that by 1680 France had a considerable naval fleet.

Colbert believed that France needed overseas colonies as a source of cheap raw materials. He purchased the islands of Guadeloupe and Martinique in the West Indies and set up armed trading posts in Africa and India. He also encouraged French settlement in Canada, in Louisiana, and on the island of Hispaniola in the Caribbean. Colbert sought French self-sufficiency—he wanted France to grow all the food and produce all the goods it needed. So he placed high tariffs on foreign products entering France and gave subsidies to French manufacturers.

Colbert held the mercantilist view that the world's supply of bullion, or treasure wealth, was limited, and so he made it illegal to export money from France. He also passed laws to encourage growth in the population of France. Men were discouraged from becoming priests (and thus from living a celibate life), and parents with large families were taxed less heavily. Thanks to Colbert's policies, France had the largest and most successful economy in Europe in the late seventeenth century.

Below The success of France under the so-called Sun King, Louis XIV, was due largely to *Colbertisme*—the mercantilist policies of his finance minister, Jean-Baptiste Colbert, shown here in a 1676 portrait by Marc Nattier.

FREE TRADE

Toward the end of the eighteenth century, the Scottish economist Adam Smith (1723–1790) developed new theories to explain the workings of national economies. A believer in free trade, in his 1776 book *Inquiry into the Nature and Causes of the Wealth of Nations,* Smith argued that a government should not interfere in its national economy. Smith also believed that a nation's wealth was measured not by the amount of money it possessed but by its ability to produce things it could sell. In the nineteenth century a free-trading Britain became the wealthiest country in the world. It seemed that Smith's theories had been proved correct, and mercantilist ideas were terminally discredited.

SEE ALSO

- Natural Resources
- Trade

MERCATOR, GERARDUS

DESPITE A HUMBLE START IN LIFE, the Flemish mapmaker Gerardus Mercator (1512–1594) became one of the greatest figures in the history of cartography. Mercator's *Atlas* was the first of its kind. It contained maps that, in terms of detail, precision, and beauty, improved significantly on those that existed beforehand. The Mercator projection is the best-known solution to the problem of representing the spherical earth on a flat map.

Below **This picture of Mercator is from the first edition of his *Atlas*, published in 1585.**

POOR BEGINNINGS

Gerardus Mercator was born Gerhard Kremer in 1512 in Flanders (part of present-day Belgium). His father was a shoemaker, and as a child, Mercator seldom had anything other than bread to eat. Nevertheless, he studied hard and by age seven could read and speak Latin. When Gerhard's father died in 1526, his uncle became his guardian and paid for his education. Gerhard changed his first name to Gerardus and his surname from Kremer (the German word for "merchant") to Mercator (the Latin for "merchant").

A CRISIS OF CONFIDENCE

In 1532 Mercator graduated from the University of Louvain with a degree in philosophy. However, he found the teachings of the ancient Greek philosopher Aristotle—the basis of all he had learned—to be in conflict with his Christian beliefs. Not knowing what he should do in life, he spent two years travel-

---

MARCH 5, 1512
Mercator is born Gerhard Kremer in Rupelmonde, Flanders.

1530
Enters the University of Louvain.

1536
Marries Barbara Schelleken, with whom he will have six children. Together with Gemma Frisius and Gaspar à Myrica, constructs a terrestrial globe.

1537
Constructs a celestial globe and publishes a map of Palestine.

1538
Publishes his first map of the world, which shows North and South America as separate continents.

1544
Is arrested and imprisoned on charges of heresy.

1552
Moves to Duisburg.

1554
Publishes a fifteen-sheet map of Europe.

1564
Publishes a wall map of the British Isles.

1567
Starts work on his *Atlas*.

1569
A Mercator projection map of the world is published for the first time.

After a great deal of self-questioning and doubt, Mercator realized that he had finally found his life's purpose in the study of geography:

Since my youth geography has been for me the primary object of study. When I was engaged in it, having applied the considerations of the natural and geometric sciences, I liked, little by little, not only the description of the earth, but also the structure of the whole machinery of the world, whose numerous elements are not known by anyone to date.

Gerardus Mercator,
Introduction to Ptolemy's *Geography* (1578)

ing restlessly throughout northern Europe. According to one story, on one occasion he walked from Louvain (present-day Leuven, Belgium) to Antwerp and back again, a distance of some sixty miles (96 km).

A SENSE OF PURPOSE

Mercator's travels had one very important effect on him: he developed an interest in geography. This science was compatible with his religious beliefs, for describing the wonders of the world was a way of celebrating God's creation. After returning to Louvain, Mercator worked as assistant to Gemma Frisius, one of Europe's leading mathemati-

Above **The title page of Mercator's *Atlas* showed the Greek god Atlas holding the earth.**

cians. Frisius had been Mercator's mathematics teacher at his university and was a very influential figure in the young man's life. The two men developed a close friendship and a common interest in cosmography, the science of mapping the universe.

1578
Within the *Atlas*, Mercator publishes updated versions of twenty-eight maps originally prepared by Ptolemy.

1585
Adds new maps of France, Germany, and the Netherlands to the *Atlas*.

1589
Adds new maps of Italy, the Balkans, and Greece to the *Atlas*.

DECEMBER 2, 1594
Dies in Duisburg.

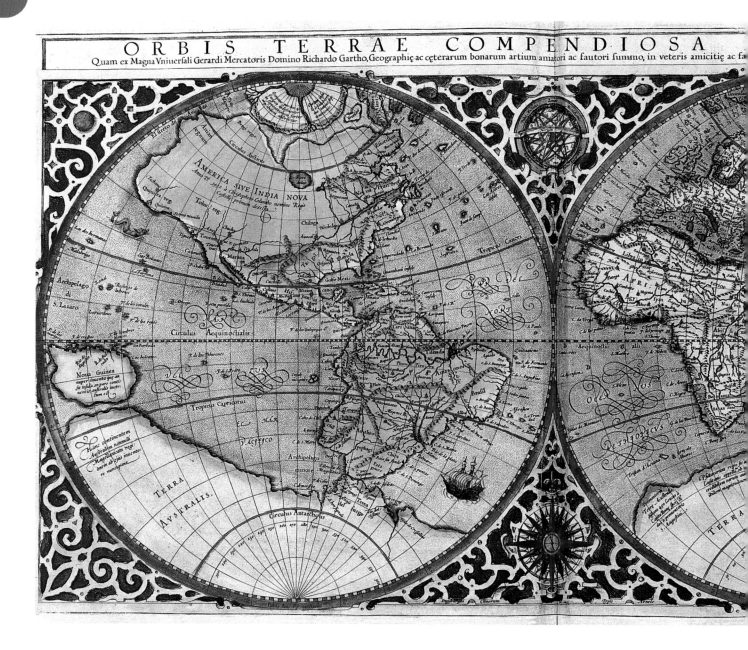

ORBIS TERRAE COMPENDIOSA

Quam ex Magna Vniuerfali Gerardi Mercatoris Domino Richardo Gartho, Geographiç ac cçterarum bonarum artium amatori ac fautori fummo, in veteris amicitiç ac fa

Above **This double hemisphere map of the world was published in Mercator's *Atlas* and was much copied during the late fifteenth and early sixteenth centuries.**

FIRST MAPS

In 1536 Mercator produced his first terrestrial globe (depicting the earth) and in 1537 his first celestial globe (depicting the stars). In 1538 he produced his first world map—the first to divide the American continent into North and South America.

In February 1544 Mercator was arrested and imprisoned for heresy (he was a Protestant in a region governed by a Catholic ruler). Burning at the stake and live burial were possible punishments for heretics, so Mercator was fortunate to be released in September of the same year.

In 1551 Mercator moved to Duisburg (in present-day Germany). By 1554, when he produced a new fifteen-sheet map of Europe, he was the leading mapmaker of his day. In 1564 he produced a map of the British Isles that surpassed all others in its detail.

THE NEED FOR A NEW PROJECTION

In the mid-sixteenth century there was no satisfactory solution to the mathematical puzzle of projecting the spherical earth onto a flat map. Mercator set about devising a new projection, and in 1569 the Mercator projection world map was published. Mercator

CRIPTIO
moriã Rumoldus Mercator fieri curabat A. M.D.Lxxxvii.

represented the world in such a way that lines of longitude and latitude were set out as straight lines in a grid. More important still, rhumb lines (lines of constant bearing) also appeared as straight lines. With this innovation, the path of a ship directed toward a single compass point would be a straight line on a Mercator map.

Mercator's projection was of inestimable value to navigators and geographers, and the great advances in mapping made over the following three centuries would have been impossible without it. Despite its distortions, the Mercator projection remains a view of the shape of the earth with which people all over the world are familiar.

THE FINAL MASTERPIECE

In the mid-1560s Mercator conceived the idea of a single work describing the whole world. In 1567 he began work on the first part, a chronology of the world from its creation to 1567. By 1578 he had added twenty-eight updated versions of maps produced by Ptolemy in the first century. In 1585 he added fifty-one new maps of France, Germany, and the Netherlands and in 1589 twenty-two modern maps of Italy, the Balkan region of southeastern Europe, and Greece. The illustration at the front of the book showed the ancient Greek god Atlas holding the earth, and thus the word *atlas* became the standard name for a book of maps. In 1590 Mercator had a stroke from which he never recovered. In 1594 he died, and the *Atlas* was completed by his son.

SEE ALSO

- Latitude and Longitude • Mapmaking
- Map Projection

MISSIONS

A MISSION IS AN ORGANIZED EFFORT by members of a religious faith to spread their beliefs and practices or to carry out humanitarian work, usually in a foreign country. From the fifteenth century, priests accompanied many voyages of conquest and discovery, especially those launched from Catholic countries. Conversion of native peoples became a major component of the process of colonization, and from the seventeenth century in North America, missionaries ventured out unaccompanied by nonmissionary explorers.

EARLY CHRISTIAN MISSIONS

Christianity is unique among religions in that its adherents are explicitly commanded to spread their faith throughout the world and to engage actively in recruiting new members (a process known as proselytizing). During the first centuries CE, Roman missionaries traveled throughout the Roman Empire to convert non-Christian peoples such as the Celts, the Goths, and the Franks.

Below **The Catholic Mission in Little Loretto, Kentucky, was founded in 1812.**

CHRISTIANITY IN THE AMERICAS

Missionary activity was not a priority on the European expeditions of the early fifteenth century; rather, the search for riches, trade routes, and new lands was uppermost in the mind of those who commissioned the voyages. Yet priests often accompanied these expeditions in order to minister to the European explorers and other crew members during the travels. Later in the century, as explorers began to travel farther afield in search of direct routes to Asia—a process that culminated in the discovery of the New World—the Roman Catholic Church took the opportunity to spread the Christian faith to newly discovered countries by giving the priests missionary duties.

In 1494, with the support of Pope Alexander VI, the Portuguese and Spanish monarchs drew up the Treaty of Tordesillas, which divided the newly discovered territories between the two nations. In return, Spain and Portugal took responsibility for introducing the peoples of their territories to Christianity. In 1533 the French king Francis I persuaded Pope Clement VII to allow France also to seek new territory in the Americas, with the proviso that France likewise undertake missionary activity in any lands it conquered.

THE COUNCIL OF TRENT

At the Council of Trent, held in northern Italy between 1545 and 1563, the Roman Catholic authorities acknowledged that the increase in

European influence around the world provided an opportunity to spread the Christian faith. The Catholic Church decided that missionary activity was to be encouraged, and priests, charged with the sole task of setting up missions and undertaking the conversion of native peoples, began to accompany voyages of exploration.

LIFE IN A COLONY

As efforts were made to expand small settlements in newly discovered lands into European colonies, missionaries were sent out as an integral part of the colonizing process. Working in a colony had its advantages. Living for longer periods in the communities they sought to Christianize, missionaries could act more like priests. They were able to spend time gaining the trust of the people they preached to and were in charge of their own

For Christians, the following passage from the New Testamant was an explicit command to engage in missionary activity:

And Jesus came and spake unto them, saying, All power is given unto me in heaven and in earth.
Go ye therefore, and teach all nations, baptizing them in the name of the Father, and of the Son, and of the Holy Ghost: Teaching them to observe all things whatsoever I have commanded you.

Matthew 28:18–20 (KJV)

work instead of simply following in the path of an explorer. Missionaries naturally sought to extend their congregation farther beyond the bounds of established colonies; in doing so, they often ended up exploring uncharted areas themselves.

Above **British Christian missionaries gained a significant foothold in China when Hong Kong was ceded to Britian in 1842. British missionary schools, such as this one in Canton, southern China (photographed in 1907), were set up with the aim of spreading Christianity among the Chinese people.**

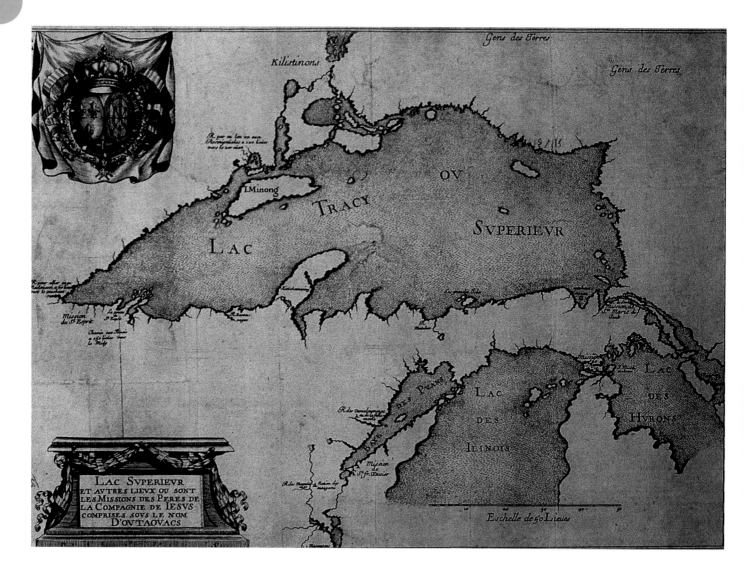

The first European map of Lake Superior, with decorative cartouche showing a royal coat of arms, inscriptions including "Gens des Terres," "Kilistinons," "LAC TRACY OV SVPERIEVR," "I.Minong," "Mission de St Esprit," "LAC DES ILINOIS," "LAC DES HVRONS," and a title cartouche reading "LAC SVPERIEVR ET AVTRES LIEVX OU SONT LES MISSIONS DES PERES DE LA COMPAGNIE DE IESVS COMPRISES SOVS LE NOM D'OVTAOVACS," with "Eschelle de 50 Lieües."

Above **The first European map of Lake Superior, published in 1672, was drawn by two Jesuits, Claude Allouez and Claude Dablon, while performing their missionary duties.**

IN THE NAME OF CHRISTIANITY

The prime motives of European explorers of the fourteenth and fifteenth centuries were territorial and commercial. Nevertheless, many explorers used religion to support their claim to the lands they discovered. They set up crosses inscribed with the name of their monarch together with religious titles, such as His Catholic Majesty and Defender of the Faith. From the early sixteenth century, all expeditions setting out from Catholic countries were obliged by a clause in their commission to take missionaries with them.

JESUIT MISSIONARIES IN CANADA

The Jesuits, members of a Roman Catholic order founded in 1534, were committed missionaries. By 1626 they had sent over 15,500 missionaries around the world—far more than any other religious order. The first missionaries to be sent to colonies in New France (present-day Canada) were two Jesuits, who arrived in Acadia in 1611. By 1625 the Jesuits were working throughout the Great Lakes region, and in 1632 Cardinal Richelieu, the French first minister, gave the Jesuits control of all missionary work in New France.

1494
Under the Treaty of Tordesillas, territory in the New World is divided between Spain and Portugal.

1533
Pope Clement VII allows France to explore the New World.

1611
The first Jesuit missionaries arrive in New France.

1632
Cardinal Richelieu gives the Jesuits control of missionary work in New France.

1647
Jean de Quen discovers and crosses Lake Piékouagami (later Lac Saint-Jean) in Canada.

1840
David Livingstone begins his travels in Africa.

Jesuits were generally very well educated, and many made significant contributions to exploration. One missionary, Father Bressani, calculated longitude by watching eclipses of the moon. Another, Jean de Quen, became the first European to discover and cross Lac Saint-Jean (in present-day Quebec) and later made a detailed record of his journey. In 1672 Fathers Claude Dablon and Claude Allouez made a chart of Lake Superior unmatched in its detail until the British hydrographic surveys of the nineteenth century.

After New France was conquered in 1763 by England—a Protestant nation—the Jesuits were withdrawn from the interior missions and forbidden to recruit members into their ranks. This ban was finally lifted in 1842.

DECLINE OF MISSIONARY EXPLORATION

Although their education enabled the Jesuits to make great contributions to world exploration in the sixteenth and seventeenth centuries, they were missionaries first and foremost, and when the nature of exploration changed during the eighteenth and nineteenth centuries, the work of the Jesuits ceased to feature prominently.

On the day he set foot in the New World, Chistopher Columbus (c. 1451–1506) pondered the likelihood of converting native peoples to Christianity:

Soon many of the islanders gathered round us. I could see that they were people who would be more easily converted to our Holy Faith by love than by coercion, and wishing them to look on us with friendship I gave some of them red bonnets and glass beads which they hung round their necks, and many other things of small value, at which they were so delighted and so eager to please us that we could not believe it. . . . They must be good servants, and intelligent, for I can see that they quickly repeat everything said to them. I believe they would readily become Christians; it appears to me that they have no religion.

Christopher Columbus, *Journal,*
October 12, 1492

Left **This pictorial catechism (a summary of religious doctrine) was used by Spanish missionaries to teach American Indians the principles of Christianity.**

Right **From the sixteenth century, the Portuguese settlement of Macao in southeastern China was an important center of Jesuit missionary activity in the Far East. This convent for the education of girls was established by Jeronymo de Matta, bishop of Macao from 1845 to 1859.**

Robert Moffat *1795–1883*

*T*he Scottish missionary Robert Moffat lived in Africa for fifty-six years and established one of the biggest Protestant missions on the continent at Kuruman (in present-day South Africa). He traveled extensively, wrote about his missionary work, and translated the Bible into the southern African Tswana language. Moffat became David Livingstone's father-in-law in 1845, when Livingstone married Moffat's daughter Mary.

With Alexander von Humboldt (1769–1859) and other such explorers came the era of the scientist-explorer. These explorers were less concerned with the discovery of new lands and more concerned with scientific observation. Members of this new breed of explorer tended to be highly trained in sciences such as botany, hydrography, metallurgy, mineralogy, and cartography. Despite their good general education, missionaries were not trained to carry out such technically demanding surveys of the places they traveled through.

EXPLORING AFRICA'S INTERIOR

The English explorer David Livingstone (1813–1873) was one of the last missionaries to make a significant impact on world exploration. Livingstone spent thirty years exploring the interior of Africa in search of a viable route across the continent. During his travels he gathered a wealth of information about the continent and its people.

SPREADING THE WORD

When the empires of Spain, Portugal, and France shrank during the eighteenth century, so did the number of Catholic missions in their territories. Nevertheless, the Catholic Church acted independently to establish new missions around the world. Jesuits continue to pursue missionary activity in the twenty-first century, as do Mormons (members of the Church of Latter-day Saints) and Protestant groups, such as Baptists and Methodists.

SEE ALSO
- Columbus, Christopher • France
- Jolliet, Louis • Kino, Eusebio Francisco
- Livingstone, David • Marquette, Jacques
- Portugal • Spain

Museums

ARCHAEOLOGISTS HAVE FOUND COLLECTIONS OF OBJECTS dating from ancient times, a fact that suggests that people have always been collectors. A museum is a place that houses collections of objects and arranges them in such a way that they may be studied by visitors. Museums originated in Europe during the fifteenth and sixteenth centuries, a period known as the Renaissance because it saw a rebirth of cultural and scientific achievement and a resurgence of interest in classical learning. The relationship between museums and exploration was a two-way process. While museums preserved, made sense of, and popularized the discoveries made by explorers, they also inspired future explorers with a sense of wonder and a yearning to explore the world.

Left **The objects, animals, and people Columbus brought back from his voyage to the Americas caused a great sensation at the Spanish court.**

Early Collections

The word *museum* comes from an ancient Greek word that denotes the place inhabited by the Muses, the nine daughters of Zeus who inspired the creative arts. The word reemerged in the fifteenth century to describe the collection of works of art and other curiosities gathered by the Florentine prince Lorenzo de Medici (1449–1492). The most prized objects for collectors of the Renaissance were relics from ancient Greece and Rome, often pillaged from their original location.

Exploration and collection have always been closely linked. Before the late nineteenth century, when for the first time technology allowed explorers to take photographs of their journeys, the only sure proof that an explorer had visited a place was if he or she brought back a memento, usually a rare or unfamiliar object. When Christopher Columbus returned from his first journey to the Americas in 1493, for example, he brought with him pieces of gold and amber, cotton, herbs, parrots, and even some native people from the islands he had visited.

In his 1565 work on collecting, *Teatrum Sapientiae* ("theater of wisdom"), the Flemish physician Samuel van Quicheberg called for collections (often known as cabinets in northern Europe) to be arranged systematically. In this way, he claimed, the whole universe could eventually be arranged and labeled.

PRESERVE, SHOW, INTERPRET

As natural and material sciences blossomed during the seventeenth and eighteenth centuries, practitioners and students developed an increasing interest in the natural world. Explorer-scientists such as Alexander von Humboldt (1769–1859) and Joseph Banks (1743–1820) brought back from their journeys a wealth of exotic specimens, whether flora and fauna, rocks and seawater, or artifacts such as weapons and jewelry. A number of new museums sprang up with a threefold purpose: to preserve evidence of the human and natural world, to display it to the public, and to interpret it. During the sixteenth century Italy boasted some 250 private

1422
Cheng Ho returns to China with African animals.

1493
Columbus returns to Spain from the Caribbean with a collection of exotic specimens.

1565
Samuel van Quicheberg describes the science of collecting in *Teatrum Sapientiae.*

1637
John Tradescant Jr. begins to collect specimens in Virginia.

1656
Publishes a catalog of his collection, which he names Museum Tradescantium.

1662
Tradescant dies.

1683
Ashmolean Museum opens.

1759
British Museum opens.

1785
Prado opens in Madrid.

1793
Louvre Museum opens in Paris.

1828
London Zoo opens to the public.

1846
Smithsonian Institution opens in Washington, DC.

Zoos

Collections of captive animals almost certainly originated in the ancient civilizations of western Asia. Egyptian tomb paintings at Saqqara, which date from around 2500 BCE, depict African antelopes wearing collars. The Chinese empress Tanki, who ruled around 1150 BCE, built a marble "house of deer," and Wen Wang, who ruled around 1000 BCE, established a so-called Garden of Intelligence, which extended some 1,500 acres (6 km²). By the fourth century BCE, collections of captive animals existed in most Greek city-states. The Macedonian general Alexander the Great (356–323 BCE) sent back to Greece many animals that were caught on his expeditions through western and central Asia. The fifteenth-century Chinese explorer Cheng Ho returned from Africa with at least one giraffe and one zebra. On his expedition to present-day Mexico (1519–1523), Hernán Cortés discovered a magnificent zoo whose collection was so large that three hundred zookeepers were required to look after it.

During the eighteenth century, European scientist-explorers brought back increasing numbers of exotic specimens from remote areas of the world. Interest in zoology bloomed, and public zoological gardens were opened in Vienna, Madrid, and Paris. London Zoo, which opened to the public in 1828, opened the world's first reptile house in 1849 and the first public aquarium (housing marine creatures) in 1853.

natural history collections. It was during this period that many Asian and American plants (the rhododendron is just one example) were introduced to Europe for the first time.

TRADESCANT'S ARK

John Tradescant (c. 1577–1638) was an English gardener, naturalist, and traveler who, after sailing to northern Russia in 1618, brought back specimens and made the first written record of Russian plants. In 1625 the Duke of Buckingham hired Tradescant "to deal with all merchants from all places, but especially from Virginia, Bermudas, Newfoundland, Guinea, the Amazon, and the East Indies, for all manner of rare beasts, fowls and birds, shells and stones." Tradescant soon built up an enormous collection of specimens from all over the world. The array of objects, housed in Lambeth, London, was so vast and comprehensive that it was popularly known as Tradescant's Ark.

Left **By the second half of the nineteenth century, zoos, such as the one in this painting by Giuseppe Barison (1853–1931), were being opened all over the world. Most modern zoos have as their aim, not the study of animals, but public entertainment.**

Above **Built from red Maryland sandstone and completed in 1855, the first building of the Smithsonian Institution is popularly known as the Castle and houses the administrative offices and information center.**

John Tradescant Jr. continued his father's work by adding to the ark with donations, purchases, and specimens he brought back from his own three visits to Virginia between 1637 and 1654. In 1656 he published a full catalog of the collection, for which his own name was Museum Tradescantium (Museum of the Tradescants). This name was the first recorded use of the word *museum* in its modern sense.

Tradescant's list of stuffed birds, fish, insects, fruits, plants, and clothes, along with an array of other objects, is a remarkable testimony to almost two centuries of European exploration. The collection even included a stuffed dodo, a bird that became extinct sometime before the end of the seventeenth century.

THE ENLIGHTENMENT AND BEYOND

During the eighteenth century, a number of factors—widespread exploration, increased global trade, and the growth of a movement glorifying rational inquiry that became known as the Enlightenment—resulted in the opening of several major museums, first in Europe and then around the world. The British Museum opened in London in 1759 when the government took over responsibility for preserving and displaying the collections and cabinets of Sir Robert Cotton, Robert Harley, Sir Hans Sloane, and William Courten. In 1793, when France's revolutionary government decided to put the royal collection on public display in Paris, the Louvre Museum was established.

The Vatican collections of the Roman Catholic Church were reorganized in the eighteenth century, and Spain's Prado Museum opened in Madrid in 1785. The wave of museum building reached a climax in the nineteenth century, when even moderate-sized towns sported collections of stuffed birds and animals from exotic places. Before the late twentieth century and the age of mass travel, the museum was a way of presenting the fruits of exploration to every inquiring European.

Perhaps the most outstanding nineteenth-century museum was the Smithsonian Institution in Washington, DC. Founded by James Smithson, an English chemist, with an initial gift of almost $500,000, its stated purpose was "the increase and diffusion of knowledge among men." It has since grown into one of the finest museums in the world and houses more than 120 million objects that represent a natural and cultural history of the world.

SEE ALSO

• Banks, Joseph • Cheng Ho

• Humboldt, Alexander von • Natural Sciences

• Smithsonian Institution

The Ashmolean Museum

*A*t their house in Lambeth, south London, John Tradescant and his son, also named John (1608–1662), assembled a vast array of animal, vegetable, and mineral specimens from around the world. Having carefully cataloged the collection during his lifetime, John Tradescant Jr. bequeathed it to his friend Elias Ashmole.

During the seventeenth century private collections and cabinets began to find their way into the public domain, a process that helped preserve the collections and offer them to a wider audience. In 1677 Ashmole passed the remarkable Tradescant collection to Oxford University as a scientific resource. The gift came with two conditions. The first was that a building be erected to house the collection. The second condition was even more significant: Ashmole stipulated that the general public have access to the collection. On May 24, 1683, the doors of the Ashmolean Musem opened. For the first time, a scientifically arranged collection was displayed for the public in its own building: the world had its first modern museum.

Left The current Ashmolean Museum building in Oxford, designed in the neoclassical style by C. R. Cockerell, was built between 1841 and 1845.

NANSEN, FRIDTJOF

FRIDTJOF NANSEN (1861–1930) LIVED A LIFE of extraordinary achievement as an explorer, a statesman, and a humanitarian. Many of his fellow countrymen consider him to be the greatest Norwegian ever to have lived. Nansen undertook two exceptional feats of Arctic exploration—the first crossing of Greenland and a voyage on his ship *Fram* across the Arctic Ocean.

Below **This photograph of Nansen, taken in 1890, captures the explorer's formidable determination.**

CROSSING GREENLAND

In 1887 Fridtjof Nansen announced that he intended to cross Greenland. This feat had never before been achieved, and to many people the plan he proposed seemed suicidal. Nansen reasoned that if he started on the east coast, a deserted wasteland of ice where there was almost no chance of rescue, he would be driven by the need to survive to head to the west coast, where there were (and still are) a handful of settlements.

For the crossing Nansen designed lightweight sleds and skis and a special cooker. Declaring that he would attain "death or the west coast," he set off with five other Norwegians on August 15, 1888, in driving storms and perilously low temperatures. The conditions were so tough that one of the men, Kristian Trana, complained, "how can people wish so much suffering on themselves that they do this?" By September 26 the party had reached the west coast. With the Arctic winter upon them, unable to travel farther

---

OCTOBER 10, 1861
Fridtjof Nansen is born in Store Froen, Norway.

1888
Leads first expedition to cross Greenland.

1893–1896
Attempts to drift to the North Pole in the *Fram*.

MARCH 14, 1895
Sets off on foot with Hjalmar Johansen to reach Pole.

APRIL 8, 1895
Turns back after reaching record latitude of 86°14′ N.

AUGUST 26, 1895
Decides to winter on Frederick Jackson Island.

MAY 19, 1896
Continues journey south.

JUNE 17, 1896
Meets up with British expedition led by Frederick Jackson.

SEPTEMBER 9, 1896
Reunited with the *Fram*, sails triumphantly into Kristiania (present-day Oslo).

1906
Is appointed Norwegian ambassador to London.

1920
Leads Norwegian delegation to League of Nations.

1922
Is awarded Nobel Peace Prize for his work for famine relief.

MAY 13, 1930
Dies in Lysaker, Norway.

The *Fram*

Designed by the Scottish boat builder Colin Archer, the 183-foot (34.5 m) *Fram* was built of seasoned oak in the shape of a giant half egg. The keel was kept small so that the ship, when ice closed around it, would rise up rather than be dragged down or crushed, as one would expect to happen. Built with both a steam engine and a full set of sails, the *Fram* also had a windmill on the deck and thus could generate its own electricity. The ship can still be seen at the Fram Museum in Bygdøy, Oslo.

Below **The *Fram*, pictured here in 1896 moored at Bergen, in southern Norway, brought Nansen international fame.**

south, the men were forced to spend the winter at the Inuit settlement of Nuuk. Nansen passed the time by making an anthropological study of the local people, which was published as *Eskimo Life* in 1889, soon after his return to Norway.

FORWARD WITH THE *FRAM*

The Greenland crossing gained Nansen considerable fame, and he began to plan an even more daring expedition. A recent American expedition to the Arctic had failed when its ship, the *Jeanette,* had sunk. Wreckage from the *Jeanette* had become trapped in the ice and drifted across the top of the world from Siberia to Greenland. This event gave Nansen the idea to construct a vessel strong enough to withstand the huge pressure of Arctic ice. He could then allow such a vessel to become deliberately trapped in the ice. The natural drift of the ice would then carry him and his ship all the way to the North Pole.

Right **Nansen deliberately allowed the *Fram* to become trapped in the ice, but when he realized that the drift of the ice would not take him all the way to the North Pole, he set out on a daring journey on foot .**

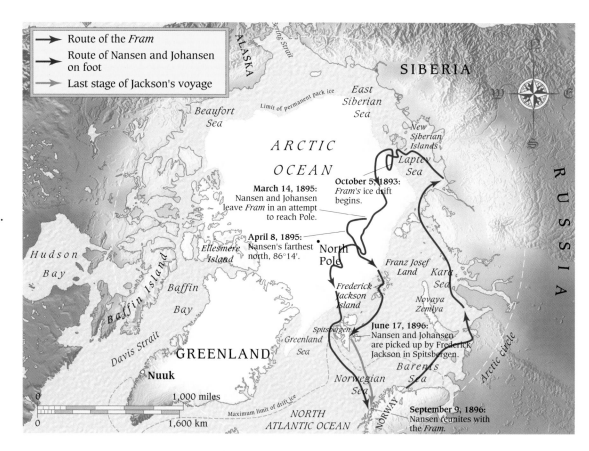

Such a voyage would take several years to complete and required uncommon dedication. Nansen's reputation ensured the support of the Norwegian government, and several private backers agreed to finance the building of a special boat, which was named the *Fram* ("forward").

The *Fram* headed north from Norway on July 21, 1893, with Nansen and twelve other men on board. Having sailed into the Northeast Passage, by October 5 the ship had become caught in the Arctic ice near the New Siberian Islands. Thus began the slow drift toward the Pole. Although the *Fram* withstood the journey magnificently, things did not go entirely as planned. By February 1895, Nansen realized that the drift of the ice was not going to take him directly to the Pole. If he wanted to get there, he would have to leave the ship and head north on foot.

He and a crewmate, Hjalmar Johansen, set out on March 14 with two kayaks, three sleds, and a team of twenty-four dogs. Less than a month later, on April 8, they were forced to turn back. The biting cold of the Arctic and a maze of pressure ridges they encountered had exhausted them. Nevertheless, the two men had reached a latitude of 86°14' N, farther north than anyone had ever traveled. Meanwhile, the *Fram*, continuing its drift through the ice, eventually broke free and returned to Norway.

STRUGGLE FOR SURVIVAL

Nansen and Johansen were way beyond any hope of rescue and had only their own wits and strength to keep them alive. Over the summer they struggled south and warded off starvation by killing and eating their dogs. They reached an island that Nansen would later name Frederick Jackson Island and in late August, as the brutal Arctic winter set in, they built a hut of stones and walrus hide. They remained in place for nine months waiting for the weather to improve so that they might resume their journey, surviving on any food they could catch—mainly walrus and polar bear meat.

On May 19, 1896, the two men headed south to Spitsbergen. They traveled through open water in an improvised catamaran constructed from their two kayaks strapped together. On June 17 they crossed the path of another polar expedition, led by the British explorer Frederick Jackson. Nansen and Johansen reached Norway just a few days before the *Fram* and were greeted as heroes.

Nansen's achievements required extraordinary strength of character:

Never stop because you are afraid . . . never keep a line of retreat: it is a wretched invention. The difficult is what takes a little time; the impossible is what takes a little longer.

Fridtjof Nansen

FURTHER TRIUMPHS

Although he never again did anything quite so daring, the rest of Nansen's life was nevertheless exceptionally eventful. He worked first as curator of zoology at Bergen Museum and later as professor of oceanography in Norway's capital, Kristiania (present-day Oslo).

In later life Nansen became a humanitarian and diplomat. He played a leading role in the establishment of a separate Norwegian state (Norway and Sweden had until then been one country) and became Norway's first ambassador to London. He led Norway's delegation at the League of Nations and was responsible for organizing the repatriation of half a million German and Austrian prisoners of war from Russia. Further work in famine relief and refugee aid contributed greatly to his reputation and won him a Nobel Peace Prize in 1922.

SEE ALSO
• Polar Exploration

Below **In this photograph of the crew of the *Fram*, Nansen is second from the right in the front row. Hjalmar Johansen, who joined Nansen in his attempt on the Pole, is in the back row at the far right.**

NARVÁEZ, PÁNFILO DE

BRAVE, ENERGETIC, AND SUPREMELY CONFIDENT of his own abilities, the ambitious Spanish conquistador Pánfilo de Narváez (c.1480–1528) used his gentlemanly charm to secure appointment to important posts but often lacked the judgment to carry out the tasks demanded of him. Narváez was sent to Mexico in 1520 to bring Hernán Cortés to heel but failed and lost an eye in the process. A second expedition—the conquest of Florida in 1527—cost him his life.

TO THE NEW WORLD

Pánfilo de Narváez was born in Valladolid in the Spanish kingdom of Castile to a family of hidalgos (members of the gentlemanly class, the lower order of nobility). During the early sixteenth century, many men of his class had fallen on hard times and were seeking to restore the land, wealth, and prestige of their family by finding their fortune in the Americas (the New World). Accordingly, Narváez went to South America as a young man and there gained some experience as a soldier and explorer. Some years later, he became one of the first Spanish settlers on the island of Jamaica.

In 1510, when he was aged thirty and married to Maria de Valenzuela, Narváez was sent by the governor of Jamaica to Cuba, where the Spanish explorer Alonso de Ojeda (1465–1515), a veteran of several important voyages to the New World, was shipwrecked and in need of rescue.

CUBA

On this voyage Narváez came into contact with Diego Velázquez (c.1460–1524), who, like Ojeda, had sailed on Christopher Columbus's second voyage to the New World (1493–1496). In 1511 Columbus's son, Diego, gave Velázquez the task of conquering Cuba for the Spanish crown. Narváez assisted Velázquez at the head of a force of archers and gained a reputation for unnecessary cruelty toward the native people. By 1514 Cuba was in the possession of Spain, and the settlements of Baracoa and Santiago were established. Havana was founded in 1519.

Velázquez sent Narváez back to Spain to discover what rewards the crown would give the conquerors of Cuba. It appears that he argued his case well, for Velázquez was made governor-general of the island and Narváez his deputy. Both were given widespread estates and urged to establish further Spanish settlements.

CORTÉS IN MEXICO

In 1518 Velázquez declared his intention to extend Spanish power to the west by establishing a settlement on the Yucatán peninsula (present-day Mexico). Among those he chose for this task was Hernán Cortés, a conquistador who had also helped in the winning of Cuba.

Velázquez soon realized that if Cortés succeeded, his glory would eclipse that of Velázquez himself. Immediately regretting his appointment of Cortés, Velázquez tried to stop the expedition. However, Cortés had foreseen this change of heart. He quickly set up his expedition, which consisted of eleven ships and about six hundred men, and left Cuba suddenly and without permission in February 1519.

Left **This portrait of Charles V on horseback dates from 1548 and was painted by one of the greatest of all Italian painters, Tiziano Vecelli (usually known as Titian).**

c. 1480
Pánfilo de Narváez is born.

1510
Sails to Cuba.

1511–1514
Assists Velázquez in the conquest of Cuba.

1516
Returns to Spain and is rewarded with honors by King Charles I.

1519
Cortés invades Mexico.

1520
Narváez, sent to replace Cortés in Mexico, is defeated and captured.

1521
Is released by Cortés.

1524
Council of the Indies is set up to administer Spain's overseas possessions.

1526
Narváez and Cabeza de Vaca are authorized to colonize Florida.

1528
The two men land in Florida; Narváez and all but four of his expedition die.

1536
Cabeza de Vaca enters Mexico City.

Showing great skill in diplomacy and great daring in battle, Cortés seized Tenochtitlán, the Aztec capital in central Mexico, in November. In March 1520 Velázquez, alarmed by Cortés's independent action, dispatched Narváez to Mexico with some nine hundred well-armed men and artillery and orders to arrest Cortés and replace him. When Cortés heard of the arrival of Narváez, he left Tenochtitlán and met Narváez in battle. Cortés defeated and captured his rival, recruited Narváez's soldiers into his own army, and resumed his conquest of Mexico.

THE FLORIDA FIASCO

In 1521, under orders from Spain, Cortés released Narváez, who returned to Spain and met Álvar Núñez Cabeza de Vaca (c. 1490–1560), an equally ambitious young explorer whose grandfather had seized the Canary Islands for Spain.

In 1526, tempted by stories of the fabulous riches to be found in Florida, King Charles I authorized Narváez and Cabeza de Vaca to attempt the conquest of that region and lands as far west as the Rio Grande. The two

men left Spain in June 1527 with five ships and around six hundred sailors, soldiers, and settlers. By the time they reached Tampa Bay in April 1528, desertions and violent storms had reduced their command to some 345 people.

Narváez tortured a local Indian chief (he cut off the man's nose) and thereby extracted a (false) confession that the Apalachee people had much gold. Narváez sent his ships on ahead, with the intention of rejoining them farther along the coast, and took a company of men on a quest for the treasure.

Disease and continual fighting steadily took their toll on the men as they continued their fruitless search for gold among the hills of northwestern Florida. Narváez's fleet waited for him in vain; his wife even hired sailors to try to find him. (One of them, Juan Ortiz, was captured by Indians and rescued by the chief's daughter; some believe their story is the true origin of the Pocahontas legend.)

DEATH AND ESTIMATION

In September 1528 Narváez finally despaired of ever being rescued or finding gold. He

Right **Álvar Núñez Cabeza de Vaca survived the series of disasters and misjudgments that killed Narváez and most of his expedition and made an almost miraculous return to Mexico City in 1536.**

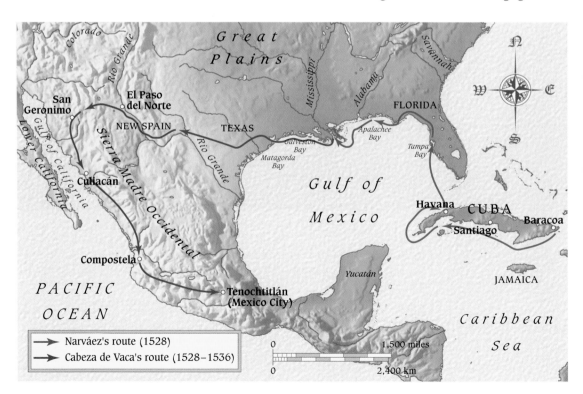

Father Olmedo, Cortés's ambassador, visited Narváez's camp on the eve of his battle with Cortés:

Narváez he described as puffed up by authority, and negligent of precautions against a foe whom he held in contempt. He was surrounded by a number of pompous, conceited officers, who ministered to his vanity, and whose braggart tones the good father [Olmedo], who had an eye for the ridiculous, imitated. . . . Many of the troops, he said, showed no great partiality for their commander, and were strongly disinclined to rupture with their countrymen.

William H. Prescott,
The Conquest of Mexico (1843)

ordered his remaining 242 men to build five boats, in which they set out for Mexico. The distance was far greater than Narváez had imagined. A storm seized the craft near the mouth of the Mississippi River, and all but eighty members of the expedition were drowned, including Narváez. The survivors tried to make their way inland but were soon captured by Indians. Only four survived.

Cabeza de Vaca was one of the survivors. He lived alone among the Indians for several years and, as a result of his medical skills, came to be revered by them as a healer. When he finally reached Mexico City in June 1536, he was accompanied by six hundred adoring followers.

SEE ALSO

• Cabeza de Vaca, Álvar Núñez • Cortés, Hernán

NASA

AN INDEPENDENT AGENCY of the United States government, the National Aeronautics and Space Administration (NASA) was established on October 1, 1958, to develop programs for the exploration of space.

THE SPACE RACE

After the open hostilities of World War II, the world entered a long period of ideological and strategic conflict know as the cold war. Broadly speaking, the cold war was fought between capitalist powers, led by the United States, and communist-governed countries, led by the Soviet Union. The two superpowers competed in many fields of endeavor, including the exploration of space. This competition became known as the space race.

In 1957, when the Soviet Union launched the first artificial satellite, *Sputnik 1*, into space, the United States responded quickly. The American satellite *Explorer 1* was launched four months later, and, less than a year after the launch of *Sputnik 1*, the U.S. government formed NASA as an independent agency dedicated to winning the space race.

MANNED SPACEFLIGHT PROGRAMS

From NASA's inception, sending humans to space was a key objective. Between 1961 and 1972, NASA undertook three major manned spaceflight programs. The Mercury program

OCTOBER 1, 1958
NASA is formed.

MAY 25, 1961
John F. Kennedy announces that the U.S. intends to put a man on the moon before the end of the decade.

1961–1963
NASA runs the Mercury program.

1965–1966
NASA runs the Gemini program.

1968–1972
NASA runs the Apollo program.

JULY 20, 1969
During the *Apollo 11* mission, Neil Armstrong and Buzz Aldrin walk on the moon.

MARCH 2, 1972
A space probe named *Pioneer 10* travels to Jupiter.

1973
The *Skylab* project enables astronauts to live in space.

APRIL 5, 1973
Pioneer 11 travels to Saturn.

1975
NASA and the Soviet Union take part in the Apollo-Soyuz Test Project. Two Viking spacecraft are launched to look for signs of life on Mars.

APRIL 12, 1981
The space shuttle takes off on its first mission.

1993
The United States and Russia agree to build the International Space Station (ISS) together.

NOVEMBER 7, 1996
Mars Global Surveyor is launched on a mission to map the surface of Mars.

was designed to find out whether a human could survive in space. The Gemini program examined how two astronauts might work together. The Apollo program was concerned with reaching and exploring the moon. Six of the eleven manned Apollo missions landed on the moon's surface, with the first touching down on July 20, 1969.

In 1962 President Kennedy spoke of his determination to succeed in the space race:

The exploration of space will go ahead, whether we join in it or not, and it is one of the great adventures of all time, and no nation which expects to be the leader of other nations can expect to stay behind in the race for space. . . . We choose to go to the moon in this decade and do the other things, not because they are easy, but because they are hard . . . because that challenge is one that we are willing to accept, one we are unwilling to postpone, and one which we intend to win, and the others, too. It is for these reasons that I regard the decision last year to shift our efforts in space from low to high gear as among the most important decisions that will be made during my incumbency in the office of the presidency.

John F. Kennedy, speaking at Rice University in Houston on September 12, 1962

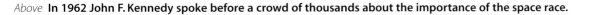

Above **In 1962 John F. Kennedy spoke before a crowd of thousands about the importance of the space race.**

SATELLITES

From the 1960s NASA developed and launched a series of satellites that were designed to remain in orbit. Early communications satellites such as *Echo, Telstar,* and *Syncom* enabled telephone and television radio waves to be transmitted reliably across great distances. Other satellites, notably *Landsat,* provided a range of statistical data.

AERONAUTICS

NASA researchers investigate airborne travel within the earth's atmosphere (aeronautics) as well as travel beyond the earth's atmosphere. NASA laboratories use a range of methods to improve the safety, reliability, and efficiency of both aircraft and spacecraft. During the 1960s NASA's X-15 program developed a rocket-powered airplane that was designed to fly above the earth's atmosphere and glide back to earth. The *X-15* provided valuable data for the space shuttle program.

THE SPACE SHUTTLE

During the 1960s and 1970s each spacecraft was used just once. In 1981 NASA completed work on the first space shuttle, a reusable spacecraft. By the end of the twentieth century, five space shuttles had completed one hundred successful spaceflights.

The space shuttle program was struck by disaster twice. On January 28, 1986, *Challenger* exploded 73 seconds after liftoff from Cape Canaveral, Florida. On February 1, 2003, seven astronauts were killed when *Columbia* broke up 200,000 feet (60 km) above Texas, fifteen minutes before the end of its sixteen-day mission.

SPACE STATIONS

In 1973 NASA launched its first manned space station, *Skylab.* Three successive teams of astronauts conducted experiments in a small workshop that orbited the earth for a total of 171 days. In 1975, under the Apollo-Soyuz program, an American and a Soviet spacecraft in orbit docked successfully, and cosmonauts and astronauts spent two days conducting experiments. In 1993 the United States, Russia, and fourteen other countries agreed to build the International Space Station (ISS) in an attempt to establish a permanent human presence in space. The ISS was able to support a permanent crew from 2000.

REMOTE CONTROL

Even the closest planets in the solar system lie at great distances from earth. At the beginning of the twenty-first century, NASA technology was not yet sophisticated enough to launch manned flights over such large distances. Instead, NASA has launched several space probes, unmanned vehicles that do not

Below **The NASA astronaut Edward White, photographed here in the cargo bay of the space shuttle** *Gemini IV,* **made the first-ever U.S. space walk in 1965.**

Above **The International Space Station (ISS) is a joint attempt, involving several nations, to establish a permanent human presence in space.**

Landsat

NASA launched its first Earth Resources Technology Satellite (ERTS), named *Landsat,* in 1972, and two more followed in 1975 and 1978. The *Landsat* satellites took photographs of the surface of the earth that were transmitted back to scientists and converted into color images. Each image covered an area equal to 115 square miles (184 km²); put together, they provided scientists with the first comprehensive view of the whole earth from space.

Later *Landsat* satellites were equipped with cameras that provided even more detailed images—they were capable of detecting any object larger than one hundred feet (30 m). *Landsat* data are used to locate natural resources, examine environmental damage, and monitor climate change.

have to be fitted with complex life-support systems and do not have to return to earth. NASA engineers have designed vehicles that can explore other planets while remaining under the control of scientists on earth. During the 1970s, the *Lunar Rover* traveled on the moon, and in 1997 the small *Pathfinder* vehicle explored the surface of Mars. In January 2004 two identical Mars rovers, *Spirit* and *Opportunity,* touched down on opposite sides of the red planet and transmitted significant new data and images back to Earth.

SEE ALSO

- Armstrong, Neil • Astronauts
- Glenn, John • Satellites
- Shepard, Alan B., Jr. • Solar System
- Space Exploration • Spacecraft

NATIVE PEOPLES

WHEN EUROPEANS FIRST ENCOUNTERED the technologically less advanced peoples of other regions of the world, their actions—whether cooperative or hostile—were characterized by a strong conviction of their own superiority. European programs of conquest and colonization were undertaken in the belief that the process of civilizing and Christianizing native peoples, whatever the cost, was politically, morally, and religiously justified. As time passed, the vast majority of Europeans came to adjust their world-view and to recognize that native peoples were human beings with rights equivalent to Europeans' own.

Above **In the 1560s French colonists encountered the Timucua, natives of Florida and Georgia. This engraving, based on a contemporary drawing by Jacques Le Moyne, shows the French involving themselves in local conflict by aiding their ally Outina against his archenemy Patanou.**

FIRST ENCOUNTERS

As the sixteenth century dawned, Spanish explorers brought back from the Americas reports of native peoples who wore little clothing, fought with spears, practiced human sacrifice, and worshiped animal gods. Some Europeans, believing humans were defined by cultural and social achievements and by an intuitive ability to accept the Christian God, were unprepared to consider the native peoples human.

NATURAL MAN

It became common during the seventeenth century to refer to native peoples as savages. Many explorers and clergymen warned that the term was inappropriate. As one Frenchman, Marc Lescarbot, observed of the Micmac peoples in 1607, "these people ... are men like ourselves ... so that if we commonly call them savages, the word is abusive and unmerited."

In fact, the root of the word *savage* is the Latin *silva* ("forest"), and thus the word was originally free from negative connotations. In

1440s
Portuguese navigators bring back first reports of native West Africans.

1492
Christopher Columbus makes the first European reports of native peoples of the Americas.

1537
The papal bull *Sublimis Deus Sic Dilexit* avers that Native Americans are human.

1577
Martin Frobisher brings three Baffin Island Inuit back to England.

1779
James Cook is killed by natives of the Hawaiian Islands.

1861
Australian aborigines try to save the lives of Burke, Wills, and King.

1888
The transatlantic slave trade is abolished.

In 1578 the French philosopher Montaigne countered suggestions that the native peoples of Brazil were savages:

I find that there is nothing barbarous and savage in this nation, by anything that I can gather, excepting, that every one gives the title of barbarism to everything that is not in use in his own country . . .

Michel de Montaigne, *Des Cannibales*

Left **The legendary wealth of Mansa Musa, king of the West African kingdom of Mali, aroused the admiration of Mediterranean cartographers, such as Gabriel Vallseca, who drew this map in the 1430s.**

ancient Greece and Rome, primitive societies, both real (as in the case of Scythia) and imagined (for example, Arcadia), were considered by many to be idyllic states where people lived according to nature, their goodness and dignity uncorrupted by civilization.

NATIVES OF THE PACIFIC ISLANDS

The theory that mankind may have degenerated rather than advanced from an earlier state gained ground during the seventeenth and eighteenth centuries. The voyages to the Pacific of James Cook (1768–1779) and Louis-Antoine de Bougainville (1766–1769), for instance, were thought to have uncovered native peoples living in an idyllic state of innocence. Bougainville, however, became disillusioned when he discovered that Tahitian society was as class ridden as that of France. In 1779 Cook himself was killed in a skirmish with some native people of the Hawaiian islands.

CHRISTIANITY AND COLONIZATION

The stated aim of colonization of the New World by Catholic Spain and Portugal in the sixteenth century was to extend the bounds of Christendom. For Catholics the benefits were both spiritual and political. Every soul converted was a soul saved, so to convert native peoples to Christianity was to carry out God's bidding. Moreover, the Catholic Church hoped to counter the military threat posed by the world's Muslim powers.

Right **The English explorer David Livingstone's exploration of the African interior during the mid-nineteenth century would have been impossible without the support, guidance, and wisdom of large teams of native people. The man pictured here ferried Livingstone across a central African river on the last day of his life.**

While Christianization was in some respects practically advantageous to native peoples (missionaries often taught their charges to read and write), many colonists used religion as a smoke screen to pursue personal wealth and prestige. This state of affairs was especially true in the New World, where native peoples often paid for Christianization with their land and freedom.

Some notable Europeans refused to accept that the right to convert native peoples to Christianity trumped the native people's own rights to their land. In 1515 the missionary Bartolomé de las Casas pleaded to the Spanish authorities for better treatment of the native peoples of the Caribbean. In 1537

Pope Paul III issued a bull, called *Sublimis Deus Sic Dilexit*, in which he declared that American Indians were "by no means to be deprived of their liberty or the possession of their property."

AFRICA AND SLAVERY

Until the fifteenth century, European contact with black Africans was extremely limited. Although aware that Africa had great civilizations, such as the kingdom of Mali, Europeans tended to characterize Africans as savages.

In the Americas the decimation of native populations by unfamiliar European diseases had created a critical shortage of labor on the plantations. The colonists solved this problem by buying enslaved Africans and taking them across the Atlantic. Between the sixteenth and nineteenth centuries, around twelve million Africans were forcibly transported to the Americas. Though certain defenders of the slave trade argued that the practice was justified because the Europeans were saving the slaves' souls, the tide of religious and secular protest at the inhumanity of the slave trade gathered momentum, and in 1888 it was finally abolished.

NATIVE EXPLORERS

Many of the great feats in the history of exploration would not have been possible without the knowledge and courage of native peoples. All major expeditions through the interior of Africa, Australia, and the Americas depended on native guides to show the way, locate sources of food and water, and negotiate with other peoples.

The exploration of Canada was propelled by the fur trade, which involved a great deal of cooperation between French and, later, English explorers and various native American peoples, including the Sioux, the Iroquois, and the Cree. Subsequent trailblazing of the western United States relied no less on the guidance of native peoples.

Many native peoples recognized that the process of colonization was dispossessing them of their lands and reacted with hostility to European explorers and the priests and missionaries who accompanied them. Australian aborigines often stalked and attacked exploration parties. On the other hand, aborigines directed Edward John Eyre to water and food on numerous occasions during his 1840 exploration of South Australia. Returning south after their crossing of Australia in 1861, Burke, Wills, and King, trapped and on the point of death in Cooper's Creek, were fed and nursed by local aborigines.

The Inuit in Elizabethan England

During his second voyage to the Canadian Arctic in 1577, Martin Frobisher (c.1535–1594) captured three Inuit (a man, woman, and child) and took them back to England, where they caused a sensation. On the Avon River in Bristol, the Inuit man used his kayak and spear to demonstrate hunting methods. He killed ducks from a great distance and showed how easily his boat could be carried through the marsh. The Inuit had little resistance to European germs, and within a month all three died, probably of pneumonia.

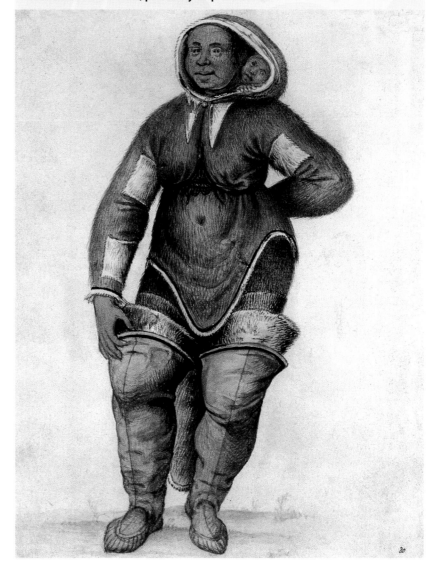

SEE ALSO

- Anthropology • Bougainville, Louis-Antoine de
- Burke, Robert O'Hara • Caravan
- Colonization and Conquest
- Cook, James • Frobisher, Martin
- Missionaries • Portugal • Spain

Above **John White, who accompanied Frobisher, drew this picture of the Inuit woman and child Frobisher captured.**

Natural Resources

PEOPLE FROM THE EARLIEST CIVILIZATIONS WERE MOTIVATED (and sometimes compelled) to venture beyond their homeland in order to find natural resources that were scarce or unavailable in their own country. In some cases one people won control of the natural resources of another by conquering and annexing the land itself. In other cases voyages of exploration led to trading agreements in which one civilization exchanged its resources for those of another. The natural resources that inspired feats of exploration included necessities, such as food and minerals, as well as luxuries, such as gold and fur.

LAND

In early societies (as in modern), one of the principal measures of wealth, prestige, and power was the amount of land that a person or people owned. In the fourth century BCE Alexander the Great launched a series of campaigns—part conquest, part exploration—that extended the dominion of his people from his native Macedon, in northern Greece, to India. In the tenth century CE the Norse, the first Europeans to reach America, sailed west across the Atlantic and, with the aim of setting up colonies in the new territory, searched for viable farmland. In the sixteenth and seventeenth centuries an increase in the population of Spain led to a shortage of land. Hundreds of hidalgos (members of the lower orders of the nobility) went to the Americas in an effort to acquire new estates and thereby boost their social standing.

FOOD

A number of voyages of exploration were launched in search of sources of food, whether everyday items, such as fish and vegetables, or luxuries, such as spices. In the sixteenth century, fishermen from northern Europe—especially southwestern England and northwestern France—sailed across the Atlantic with the aim of farming the abundant cod of North American waters.

SPICES

For Europeans, the food resources of Asia, particularly the spices of Southeast Asia, were long considered luxuries, prized not just for their taste and scent but also for their preservative qualities. From ancient times until the sixteenth century, goods were transported by land. The trade was controlled by a network of Arab merchants who obtained the goods from Asia and passed them to Europe.

---

c. 1470 BCE
The Egyptian pharaoh Hatshepsut sends ships in search of African luxuries along the Red Sea coast.

c. 450 BCE
Searching for tin, Himilco, a Carthaginian seafarer, reaches perhaps as far as Cornwall in southwestern England.

1488
The Portuguese explorer Bartolomeu Dias becomes the first European to round the Cape of Good Hope (at the southern tip of Africa).

1492
Christopher Columbus sights America; in the following decades, hundreds of Spanish and Portuguese explorers join the quest for American land and riches.

1497
The English sailor John Cabot discovers that the waters of Newfoundland (North America) are teeming with cod.

The Spice Islands

The spices valued most highly in Europe came from a group of tiny and remote tropical islands, now called the Moluccas (in Indonesia), that were known for hundreds of years as the Spice Islands. On the Spice Islands were found the extraordinarily expensive mace, nutmeg, and cloves. Strongly scented cloves, the buds of a rare tree of the myrtle family, were harvested only on Ceram, Ambon, Tidore, and Ternate. Nutmeg and mace grew only on the volcanic Banda Islands.

Right **This drawing of Europeans trading spices in the Moluccas comes from the 1555** *Cosmographie Universelle* **by Guillaume le Tetsu (c. 1509–1573).**

1531
On his third journey in search of Incan gold in South America, the Spanish explorer Francisco Pizarro conquers Peru.

1603–1608
French colonists establish the first Canadian fur-trading posts along the Saint Lawrence River.

1930s
Oil prospectors make geological surveys of the Middle East

July 4, 1997
Sojourner transmits the first photographs of the surface of Mars.

The Portuguese explorer Vasco da Gama, who sailed to India between 1497 and 1499, bought 112 pounds (51 kg) of pepper for three ducats in the Indian port of Calicut. The same quantity cost eighty ducats in Venice. With such vast profits to be made from the spice trade, the search for a direct route from Europe to Asia—and thus for control of the trade—was a major factor behind the great endeavors of European explorers during the Age of Discovery and after. At first, navigable routes were sought around the southern tip of Africa and of South America. European powers later expended vast resources on a quest for a northwest passage to Asia via North America or a northeast passage via Russia. The subsequent settling of European territories in the Americas, Africa, and Asia itself was a by-product of this process.

MINERALS

The search for minerals inspired some of the earliest recorded journeys of exploration. As the use of bronze, an extremely useful alloy made from copper and tin, spread throughout the Mediterranean, traders were forced to search farther afield for sources of tin, a scarce resource in their own countries. The voyage of Himilco in the fifth century BCE resulted in the addition of the British Isles to the map of the known world.

Later, the detailed exploration of central Africa and other areas was inspired partly by the search for valuable metals, such as copper. Likewise, the search for fresh supplies of hardwoods, such as mahogany and teak, led to the exploration and mapping of the tropical regions of Asia and South America.

During the twentieth century the search for reserves of oil produced the first detailed surveys of Arabia and of huge areas of the seabed, particularly in and around Indonesia. The exploration of Antarctica during the twentieth century was backed partly by those who hoped to exploit any mineral resources that might be found there. Fortunately for the ecology of the region, international agreements drawn up in 1959, 1980, and 1991 outlawed the exploitation of Antarctica's mineral resources.

The possible discovery of vast reserves of mineral wealth is often suggested as a justification for the huge expense of space exploration, and there are those who believe that one day humans will begin mining asteroids and even other planets.

GOLD, SILVER, AND JEWELS

Ancient Egyptians explored East Africa by land and by sea in their quest for luxuries not available in their homeland. Around 1470 BCE Hatshepsut, the female pharaoh of Egypt, launched a voyage of exploration along the Red Sea to the land of Punt (the coast of present-day Somalia). The ships returned laden with luxuries, including jewels, ivory, ebony, ointments used for religious and cosmetic purposes, and the skins of wild animals, such as leopards.

The Search for Gold

During the sixteenth century stories of gold in the Americas abounded, and myth and reality soon became indistinguishable. Pánfilo de Narváez (c.1480–1528) and Francisco Vásquez de Coronado (c.1510–1554) were only two of countless Spanish explorers who searched fruitlessly for nonexistent treasure in North America. Many died in the quest for Eldorado, a fabulous country of gold believed to be located in South America.

Similarly, when diamonds were discovered in southern Africa in the nineteenth century, stories began to circulate of further buried riches. In 1885 the writer H. Rider Haggard successfully wove this myth into one of the most exciting adventure stories of Victorian England, *King Solomon's Mines*.

Right **This painting from Hatshepsut's magnificent mortuary temple shows soldiers carrying incense trees in baskets during their expedition to Punt.**

From the seventeenth century, the market for furs prompted the exploration of Canada and Russia, while explorers looking for diamonds covered huge areas of southern Africa. The exploration of the Americas was inspired in part by a hunt for gold and silver. The speed with which South and Central America were explored after the initial forays of Hernán Cortés, Francisco Pizarro, and others was due in no small measure to the fact that the south was rich in silver. The conquest of North America, whose mineral resources were not as valuable, took longer.

Marco Polo (1254–1324) reported with amazement the gold, silver, and silks to be found in China. His writings inspired generations of European sailors, who gave names to places in Africa they passed en route—the Gold Coast, the Ivory Coast, Guinea (the name of a gold coin)—names that reflected what was uppermost in their minds.

In 1530 the secretary of Francisco Pizarro, the Spanish conqueror of Peru, described the wealth of the Inca king:

Atahualpa . . . said to the Governor [Pizarro], "I will give gold enough to fill a room twenty-two feet long and seventeen wide, up to a white line which is halfway up the wall." The height would be that of a man's stature and a half. He said that, up to that mark, he would fill the room with different kinds of golden vessels, such as jars, pots, vases, besides lumps and other pieces. As for silver, he said he would fill the whole chamber with it twice over.

Francisco de Xeres, *Narrative of the Conquest of Peru*

SEE ALSO

- Colonization and Conquest
- Columbian Exchange • Columbus, Christopher
- Coronado, Francisco Vásquez de
- Cortés, Hernán • Gama, Vasco da
- Mercantilism • Narváez, Pánfilo de
- Polo, Marco • Silk Road • Trade
- Underground Exploration
- Underwater Exploration

GLOSSARY

aeronautics The study and practice of travel through the air.

alloy A metal made of a mixture of two or more other metals; bronze, for example, is an alloy of copper and tin.

altitude Height above the surface of the earth.

amber A fossil resin of yellow-orange color.

atmosphere The layers of gases surrounding a planet.

bearing The relationship of one point to another on the earth's surface. The bearing of point *B* from point *A* is the angle between the lines *AB* and *AN*, where *N* is any point due north of *A*.

braggart A loud and arrogant boaster.

cartography The science and art of mapmaking.

catamaran A ship or boat that has two hulls and is therefore difficult to capsize.

celestial Of or relating to the skies, stars, and heavens.

crane A large long-legged bird.

dodo A large flightless bird, similar to a turkey, that lived on the island of Mauritius but is now extinct.

ducado A Spanish monetary unit, equivalent to 1.33 ounces (37.6 g) of gold; also known as a ducat.

ebony A dark, hard, heavy wood.

Enlightenment An intellectual movement of eighteenth-century Europe that rejected traditional social, political, and religious arrangements and ideas in favor of new ones more closely based on logic, reasoning, and scientific observation.

heresy A belief that runs counter to an official teaching of a church or, for that matter, to a dominant opinion in a society or a state.

hidalgo A member of the lower Spanish nobility.

incumbency The period of time during which an official position, such as the presidency of a country, is held.

keelboat A shallow, covered riverboat, generally used for freight, that is usually rowed or towed.

meltwater Water that swells a river after the melting of snow and ice in mountainous regions near the river's source.

patron Someone who financially supports another person or a project.

pillage To plunder a place, that is, to remove, often violently, everything from it of material value.

pioneer The first person to attain a given goal, such as a feat of exploration, the settlement of a new territory, or the invention of a new technology.

pirogue A small boat, much like a canoe.

portage The carrying of boats overland from one waterway to another.

pressure ridge A layer of ice forced up into a block by the pressure of surrounding ice.

principality A state ruled by a prince.

recoup To receive an amount of goods or money equivalent to an amount lost.

Renaissance Literally, "rebirth"; an artistic movement that began in the fourteenth century in Italy and lasted into the seventeenth century. The Renaissance was marked by a flowering of artistic and literary achievement and a resurgence of interest in the values of ancient Greece and Rome.

space probe An unmanned, exploratory spacecraft.

terrestrial Of or relating to the earth.

trigonometry The branch of mathematics concerned with the properties of triangles.

INDEX